ACCENTS ON SHAKESPEARE

General editor: TERENCE HAWKES

Philosophical Shakespeares

Shakespeare continues to articulate the central problems of our intellectual inheritance. The plays of this Renaissance playwright still seem to be fundamental to our understanding and experience of modernity.

Key philosophical questions concerning value and meaning continue to resonate in Shakespeare's work. In the course of rethinking these issues, *Philosophical Shakespeares* actively encourages the growing dissolution of boundaries between literature and philosophy. The approach throughout is interdisciplinary, and ranges from problem-centred readings of particular plays to more general elaborations on the significance of Shakespeare in relation to individual thinkers or philosophical traditions.

Contributors: Michael D. Bristol, Stanley Cavell, Howard Caygill, Linda Charnes, Hugh Grady, David Johnson, John J. Joughin, Scott Wilson.

John J. Joughin is Senior Lecturer in English at the University of Central Lancashire. He is the editor of *Shakespeare and National Culture* (1997).

ACCENTS ON SHAKESPEARE
General Editor: TERENCE HAWKES

It is more than twenty years since the New Accents series helped to establish 'theory' as a fundamental and continuing feature of the study of literature at undergraduate level. Since then, the need for short, powerful 'cutting edge' accounts of and comments on new developments has increased sharply. In the case of Shakespeare, books with this sort of focus have not been readily available. **Accents on Shakespeare** aims to supply them.

Accents on Shakespeare volumes will either 'apply' theory, or broaden and adapt it in order to connect with concrete teaching concerns. In the process, they will also reflect and engage with the major developments in Shakespeare studies of the last ten years.

The series will lead as well as follow. In pursuit of this goal it will be a two-tiered series. In addition to affordable, 'adoptable' titles aimed at modular undergraduate courses, it will include a number of research-based books. Spirited and committed, these second-tier volumes advocate radical change rather than stolidly reinforcing the status quo.

IN THE SAME SERIES

Philosophical Shakespeares

Edited by
JOHN J. JOUGHIN

London and New York

First published 2000
by Routledge
11 New Fetter Lane,
London EC4P 4EE

Simultaneously published
in the USA and Canada
by Routledge
29 West 35th Street,
New York, NY 10001

Routledge is an imprint of the
Taylor & Francis Group

© 2000 Selection and editorial matter, John J.
Joughin; individual chapters, the respective
contributors

Typeset in Baskerville by
RefineCatch Ltd,
Bungay, Suffolk
Printed and bound in Great Britain by
TJ International Ltd,
Padstow, Cornwall

British Library Cataloguing in Publication
Data
A catalogue record for this book is available from the
British Library

Library of Congress Cataloguing in
Publication Data
A catalog record for this book has been applied for

ISBN 0–415–17388–4 (hbk)
ISBN 0–415–17389–2 (pbk)

In memory of Francis Barker
1952–1999

Contents

Contributors

Michael D. Bristol Professor of English, McGill University, Montréal

Stanley Cavell Walter M. Cabot Professor of Aesthetics and the Theory of Value, Harvard University

Howard Caygill Professor of Cultural History, Goldsmiths College, University of London

Linda Charnes Associate Professor of English, Indiana University, Bloomington

Hugh Grady Professor of English, Beaver College, Pennsylvania

David Johnson Lecturer in Literature, The Open University, Milton Keynes

John J. Joughin Senior Lecturer in English, University of Central Lancashire, Preston

Scott Wilson Senior Lecturer in English, Lancaster University

Bibliographical note

Fuller references to works mentioned throughout the volume are appended in the Bibliography.

References to Shakespeare's texts throughout are to the Arden editions of individual plays unless otherwise indicated.

General editor's preface

In our century, the field of literary studies has rarely been a settled, tranquil place. Indeed, for over two decades, the clash of opposed theories, prejudices and points of view has made it more of a battlefield. Echoing across its most beleaguered terrain, the student's weary complaint 'Why can't I just pick up Shakespeare's plays and read them?' seems to demand a sympathetic response.

Nevertheless, we know that modern spectacles will always impose their own particular characteristics on the vision of those who unthinkingly don them. This must mean, at the very least, that an apparently simple confrontation with, or pious contemplation of, the text of a 400-year-old play can scarcely supply the grounding for an adequate response to its complex demands. For this reason, a transfer of emphasis from 'text' towards 'context' has increasingly been the concern of critics and scholars since World War II: a tendency that has perhaps reached its climax in more recent movements such as 'New Historicism' or 'Cultural Materialism'.

A consideration of the conditions – social, political, or economic – within which the play came to exist, from which it derives, and to which it speaks will certainly make legitimate demands on the attention of any well-prepared student nowadays. Of course, the serious pursuit of those interests will also inevitably start to undermine ancient and inherited prejudices, such as the supposed distinction between 'foreground' and 'background' in literary studies. And even the slightest awareness of the pressures of gender or of race, or the most cursory glance at the role played by that strange creature 'Shakespeare' in our cultural politics, will reinforce a similar turn towards questions that sometimes appear scandalously 'non-literary'. It seems clear that very different and unsettling notions of the ways in which literature might be addressed can hardly be avoided. The worrying truth is that nobody can just pick up Shakespeare's plays and read them. Perhaps – even more worrying – they never could.

The aim of *Accents on Shakespeare* is to encourage students and teachers to explore the implications of this situation by means of an engagement with the major developments in Shakespeare studies over recent years. It will offer a continuing and challenging reflection on those ideas through a series of multi- and single-author books which will also supply the basis for adapting or augmenting them in the light of changing concerns.

Accents on Shakespeare also intends to lead as well as follow. In pursuit of this goal, the series will operate on more than one level. In addition to titles aimed at modular undergraduate courses, it will include a number of books embodying polemical, strongly argued cases aimed at expanding the horizons of a specific aspect of the subject and at challenging the preconceptions on which it is based. These volumes will not be learned 'monographs' in any traditional sense. They will, it is hoped, offer a platform for the work of the liveliest younger scholars and teachers at their most outspoken and provocative. Committed and contentious, they will be reporting from the forefront of current critical activity and will have something new to say. The fact that each book in the series promises a Shakespeare inflected in terms of a specific urgency should ensure that, in the present as in the recent past, the accent will be on change.

Terence Hawkes

Foreword
STANLEY CAVELL

A book entitled *Philosophical Shakespeares*, in the places I have spent the bulk of my life (primarily in the philosophy departments of two good American universities, with certain ventures into the teaching of what is called literature), is as apt to cause impatience as it is to provoke interest. Here philosophers and those concerned with the criticism and theory and history of literature still, in the main, treat each other professionally with indifference or suspicion. In the 'other' tradition of philosophy (poorly characterized as 'Continental'), and in cultures where philosophy is as much a recognized part of what it means to be educated as is the knowledge of the national literary classics, the intersection of philosophy and literature may be taken in stride, but perhaps only out of a borrowed sophistication. I imagine that a point of my composing prefatory words for the welcome appearance of an enterprise directed from this intersection that takes its audience in the first instance to be Anglo-American in training (if partly in training to resist the training's claims to exclusiveness) is to attest, as one who has chronically found himself in these precincts over the past three decades, that the enterprise is surprisingly survivable. Indeed that the time is passing in which the onslaught of literary theory in these decades served mostly to exacerbate the mutual distrust of philosophical and literary studies. The collection before us should help to hasten another time.

The issue of Shakespeare's uniqueness keeps coming up, here as elsewhere, as cause both for acclaim and for dismay, together with a repeatedly documented cause for alarm concerning the indiscriminate appropriation of Shakespeare to underwrite, or to neutralize, cultural and political oppression. I suppose I am to be counted among those who take Shakespeare's 'position' here as indeed a matter of his appropriability, as when Brecht shows us how to consider the opening scene of *Coriolanus* from the side of the rebellious populous. Such inspirations to appropriation, or counter-appropriation, point a way to articulate our persistent, or recurrent, intuition of Shakespeare's all-too-superhuman 'humanity'. I imagine this emphasis is prompted by, and finds ratification in, the perception of our age, in the theatre of the West, as one less of innovation in the composing of plays (and operas) than originality in their productions or readings, our unpredicted reconsiderations of works from any period. (Does this perception go with an idea of when this age is supposed to have begun – was it with the sense that the works of Brecht and Beckett, and the instances of Debussy's *Pelleas and Melisande*, and of *Wozzeck*, and of *Moses and Aron* have no successors to match their magnitude?) The idea of appropriability is not meant to prejudge the degree to which lines, scenes, plays may resist certain appropriations less or more than others. It is rather to make the matter of such resistance paramount in assessing cultural position, and to make the measuring of resistance a matter of critical and theatrical experimentation. (How far can any, let's say, humanizing of the character of Shylock dispel the chronic ugliness of his consciousness? How far can any visions of majesty erase the knowledge of what royalty in *Macbeth*, on both sides, is given to say and to do?) This will understand a work's measure of resistance to its culture, which may be zero, to be a measure of the culture's resistance to itself.

In the meantime I remain impressed by certain philosophical obsessions with the immeasurable magnitude of the achievement called Shakespeare's. I had occasion a few years ago to note that both Wittgenstein's rather offhand notebook entries about Shakespeare (published in a selection of such as it were extra-philosophical entries under the title *Culture and Value*) and Emerson's modest chapter about the Bard in *Representative Men* reveal, with a little pressing, certain of the most pervasive of each of these thinkers' philosophical preoccupations, or anxieties. As though it is in the call of the immense intelligence of the Shakespearean corpus that philosophy may be enabled to confess itself.

Wittgenstein's few dozen sentences on Shakespeare consist of general remarks that concern his suspicion of the way Shakespeare is conventionally praised and express his belief that Shakespeare's uniqueness is traceable to his being a '*creator of language*' rather than a poet (Wittgenstein 1994: 84), confessing that he understands how someone can call what Shakespeare creates supreme art but that he doesn't like it. Wittgenstein's expression of taste is of interest only to the extent that Wittgenstein is independently of interest. Since he is of interest to me, I wish to understand why he feels called upon to confess his (dis)taste. Take the concept of creation in its opposition to the concept of chaos and hear Wittgenstein say, from the same selection two years earlier: 'When you are philosophizing you have to descend into the old chaos and feel at home there' (65). He is evidently characterizing his late way of bringing words back to their homes, their home language games, back to the order he calls the ordinary, back, as if anew, from chaos. If this is philosophy's creativity, say it is discovering language's own creativity, then it is open to language to be discovered further, further than bringing words home as Wittgenstein's language games discern home. I surmise that what Wittgenstein senses in Shakespeare's language is the continuous threat of chaos clinging to his creation, an anxiety produced as the sense that it is something miraculous that words can mean at all, that there are words.

Emerson's general declarations about Shakespeare, like Wittgenstein's, start off with a certain studied blandness, as for example: 'Shakespeare's principal merit may be conveyed in saying that he of all men best understands the English language, and can say what he will' (Emerson 1883: 20–1). But they also in a further light turn a different physiognomy. The implication in the present case is that the rest of us are in various states of ignorance of our language and are unable to say what we will, as if we are all to some extent aphasic (which is something Lacan almost says). Emerson interprets the 'greatness' of the figures he chooses as their representativeness, and finds the importance of such representativeness in its power to emancipate. That which Shakespeare's language emancipates us from, Emerson quite explicitly describes as melancholy, idolatry, entrapment in the views of others, and blindness to the existence of others. These are a fair set of predicates of my presentation over the years of philosophical scepticism.[1]

There are readers of literature who take the view – it is, I believe, counter to the views implicit in the various procedures of the contributors to the present volume – that to derive such thoughts from texts such as Shakespeare's is to evince a blindness to, even a denial of, the very literariness of those texts, the particular interaction of the specific words of which the texts are woven. I must, of course, insist that it is precisely those very words that inspire those derivations; but, of course, that is only to be shown in specific critical interventions. Perhaps, though, for some it may seem easy to imagine that the likes of Wittgenstein and Emerson, busy with their speculations, are not attentive to, nor even interested in, the textuality of Shakespearean texts. I suppose this must be less easy to imagine in the case, for example, of Henry James. In two late texts the novelist raises what is for him the philosophically tormenting question of finding the man Shakespeare, about whom we know so little, in the poet of that name, who (as I might draw out James's perplexity), having in effect expressed himself more amply than any other human being, has given us in principle ampler evidence of his identity than any other.

In the story 'The birthplace', James writes a satirical fable about the search for the biographical facts of the Supreme Author (unmistakably identified, or deified, as Shakespeare), giving it to the chief character to say of such literalism, 'They've killed Him . . . They kill Him every day' (James 1964: 440). I find it hard to believe that the Nietzschean sentiment and phrasing are accidental. And it strikes me as the most fruitful understanding of the idea of the death of the author that I am aware of. And in an introduction two or three years later to *The Tempest*, for Sydney Lee's edition of a complete Shakespeare, James is still at it, seamlessly, at the close of his contribution:

> The secret that baffles us being the secret of the Man, we know, as I have granted, that we shall never touch the Man *directly* in the Artist. We stake our hopes thus on indirectness, which may contain possibilities; we take that very truth for our counsel of despair, try to look at it as helpful for the Criticism of the future. That of the past has been too often infantile; one has asked one's self how it *could*, on such lines, get at him. The figured tapestry, the long arras that hides him, is always there, with its immensity of surface and its proportionate underside. May it not then be but a question, for the fullness of time, of the finer weapon, the sharper point, the stronger arm, the more extended lunge?
> (James 1981: 310)

Evidently what James describes at the beginning of his introduction as 'our strained and aching wonder' (297) over this man is not to do with the small number of facts about his life we have to work with. No set of facts could themselves alleviate our ignorance. For our 'persistent ignorance', which it is 'the effect of the Plays and Poems, taken in their mass . . . to appear to mock', is an ignorance not of this man's life but of 'so many conditions of their birth' (297), that is, the birth of the works. The 'Criticism of the future' James calls for (which, unlike the infantile criticism of the past, stands to reveal these conditions) will not explain how a particular historical figure came to produce these works, but will (also, everywhere) consider how anything we understand as a finite mind could be capable of them, of composing them or reading them. Then why is the future criticism portrayed by James in the violent image of Hamlet's thrusting through his mother's tapestry?

Is the portrait simply to recognize the necessary violence, or partiality, in any critical appropriation, including that of genteel familiarity? Or isn't it also to ask us to reflect upon the violence of the appropriation the text exacts upon our attention, its attack upon our prepossessions, our pre-occupations with what we think we know about what our intellectual or cultural fathers and mothers have instilled in us, which will mean to learn how to enquire without dispatching the object of our enquiry, how to be capable of blank astonishment at how the world goes, and at the power sometimes of the art it inspires to withstand that astonishment, or name it. This seems to me a reasonable way to think about how the knowledge of the existence of other minds is to be achieved, or said otherwise (to record one of my own favourite preoccupations), how sceptical annihilation of others is to be unseated. Who more than Shakespeare have we ever thought could teach more about this?

Note

1 These two paragraphs taking up Wittgenstein's and Emerson's responses to Shakespeare owe a good deal to my paper on 'Skepticism as iconoclasm'; see Cavell 1998: 231–47.

Philosophical Shakespeares: an introduction

JOHN J. JOUGHIN

I Shakespeare and philosophy

> Thou art a scholar, speak to it, Horatio.
> (*Hamlet* I. i. 45)

Promoting a recent international sporting fixture between England and France, the BBC playfully juxtaposed a series of sound-bites from Descartes, Rousseau and Sartre alongside the more mundanely practical advice which resonated in a voice-over drawn deep from the shires of middle England: 'don't worry lads – actions speak louder than words'. The application of native common sense versus the verbose abstraction of the Continent: practice ousting theory. The implicit message was clear enough: philosophy and the British somehow constitute odd bedfellows – at best an aberration, at worst a potential source of conflict to be overcome. The place of literature in the national psyche often does not fare any better, and in its British context, Shakespeare is sometimes discussed in terms of distinctions of fine taste and so on, which have more in common with judgements concerning wine tasting or gourmet cuisine than aesthetics.

In contrast, amidst the various intellectual traditions which constitute Continental philosophy, a theoretical interest in the importance of literature to modern thought is taken as read. Indeed, literary and artistic works are fully embedded within an intellectual inheritance which regards an appreciation of literature and an understanding of the 'nature of art' as reciprocally entwined with philosophy, or, at the very least, encourages a dialogue between the two.[1] This is especially the case as far as Shakespeare is concerned, and respected thinkers such as Nietzsche, Wittgenstein and more recently Levinas and Derrida, each have had something outspoken to say about the playwright. The gap between intellectual cultures is striking, so that, as Stanley Cavell has observed:

> English philosophy is characterized, in distinction from, say, that of France and of Germany, by its relative distance from the major literature of its culture. Compared with Kant's or Hegel's or Schelling's awareness of Goethe or Hölderlin (or Rousseau or Shakespeare) or with Descartes's and Pascal's awareness of Montaigne, Locke's or Hume's or Mill's relation to Shakespeare and Milton or Coleridge (or Montaigne) amounts to hardly more than that to more or less serious hobbies, not to the recognition of intellectual competitors, fellow challengers of intellectual conscience.
>
> (Cavell 1987: 2)

Yet, in some sense of course, even when Shakespeare is confined within the formative constraints of his own intellectual tradition, the implicit philosophical significance of the playwright's work ensures that he continues to be the literary exception which proves the rule. As early as 1711, Shakespeare stands as representative of a type of native intellect, which is sufficiently well established within the context of an emergent public sphere for one commentator to label him 'the Genius of our Isle' (Vickers 1995, vol. 2: 265).[2] In Britain, as elsewhere, the playwright gradually emerges as the thinking person's thinker: an impression amply reinforced by the statue of Hamlet which stands at the centre of 'Shakespeare country' near the Royal Shakespeare Theatre at Stratford and has him at one with abstraction, posing à la Rodin as *The Thinker* – his contemplative gaze fixed on the *memento mori* of a skull, presumably itself, as Graham Holderness points out, a confused allusion to the import of the gravedigger's scene V. i. (cf. Holderness 1987: 9–12). Unsurprising then that Cavell qualifies his own observation with the 'insistence' that:

> Shakespeare could not be who he is – the burden of the name of the greatest writer in the language, the creature of the greatest ordering of English – unless his writing is engaging with the depth of the philosophical preoccupations of his culture.
>
> (Cavell 1987: 2)

Yet, while Shakespeare may be crucially 'engaged' with central questions concerning cultural and intellectual inheritance, he is *not*, by the same token, reducible to them. It follows that, even though it has continued to ensure Shakespeare's survival, the philosophical engagement to which Cavell alludes is not something one can easily quantify or readily evaluate. Indeed, insofar as Shakespeare 'preoccupies' us he often does so in ways and forms which are barely perceptible. The 'ordering of English' that Cavell refers us to is so deeply entrenched that it extends to the particles of grammar which constitute Shakespearean syntax itself, and which shelters a type of proverbial wisdom which is so thoroughly assimilated within spoken English that its provenance is customarily mislaid. One is reminded of the apocryphal story of the American tourists who catch a performance of *Hamlet* at Stratford only to complain that 'Shakespeare's full of clichés'.

All this is not to say that Shakespeare serves as a universal fount of knowledge. In fact, what is striking about many of these vestigial remainders – 'reason not the need', 'though this be madness . . . there is method in't', 'nothing will come of nothing' and so on – is their resistance to straightforward construal. In tracking back across Shakespeare's critical heritage and dipping into the closely contested editorial squabbles of years gone by, one unearths a series of textual disputes and dilemmas which open out onto questions which remain unanswered to this day. The bewilderment of those who witness the unlikely resurrection of Hermione at the end of *The Winter's Tale*, or who remain puzzled concerning the whereabouts of Lady Macbeth's 'missing children', is that they experience a form of inexplicable otherness which exceeds their intellectual grasp, rather than providing the grounded repleteness of a meaningful solution. In short, it is precisely in revealing the limits of our truth-claims that Shakespeare remains significant. And the same could be said on a broader scale of the plays themselves which, despite numerous attempts to limit or contain them, still remain meaningful in vastly different forms today than they ever did in the past.

Paradoxically, it is this evolving qualitative newness of Shakespeare's plays which ensures that they somehow remain 'representative' of our most traditional concerns. In placing Shakespeare as foremost in his pantheon of 'Representative Men' (*sic*), the nineteenth-century poet and philosopher Ralph Waldo Emerson writes:

> he [Shakespeare] wrote the text of modern life . . . He is inconceivably wise; the others, conceivably. A good reader can, in a sort, nestle into Plato's brain and think from thence; but not into Shakespeare's. We are still out of doors. For executive faculty, for creation, Shakespeare is unique. No man can imagine it better.
>
> (Emerson 1883: 201–2)[3]

Allowing for the flourish of Emerson's prose, this is not the naive or sentimental antiquarian endorsement of Shakespeare's greatness that it first
appears to be. Reading between the lines of Emerson's evaluation, it is
possible to glimpse his appreciation of the fact that the playwright's singularity is a striking blend of the familiar and the 'hitherto unthought',[4] possessing a quality which Freud characterizes as *unheimlich* or unhomely; so
that, as Emerson himself puts it, with Shakespeare 'we are still out of
doors'. The 'inconceivable' creative faculty to which Emerson alludes is a
constantly changing process which is fully enmeshed within the broader
cultural production of the 'meaning' of literary texts. And in this respect, as
Derek Attridge recently reminds us, the private innovation of 'artistic creation' needs to be construed in direct relation to its potential to transform a
reader's response within the public domain:

> it is important to acknowledge that creation always takes place in a
> culture, not just in a mind . . . innovative mental acts produce lasting
> alterations in the subjectivity that achieves them: once I have articu-
> lated the new thoughts that I had dimly apprehended, my thinking will
> never be entirely the same again. If that new articulation becomes
> public, with the disarticulation of settled modes of thought that made
> it possible (and thus that it made possible), it may alter cognitive
> frameworks across a wider domain, allowing further acts of creativity
> in other minds. This sequence of events is familiar in many fields,
> including philosophy, the sciences, politics, religion, and art.
>
> (Attridge 1999: 22–3)

It is easy enough to dismiss notions of Shakespeare's indigenous genius as
a constructed fallacy, a residue of the transcendental baggage we shed long
ago – the bankrupt legacy of a Romanticized Shakespeare which so much
recent work in cultural and literary studies has helped to dislodge. Yet, as
Attridge's remarks serve to suggest, artistic creativity is crucially implicated
in producing new forms of social interaction and in helping us to modify the
criteria by which we understand their significance. In its wider cognitive
context, this disseminative dimension of literary texts constitutes its own
form of inventiveness. It is precisely because Shakespeare's work constantly
invites and rewards changing modes of theoretical analysis that it has served
to sharpen the focus of key paradigm shifts within literary criticism over a
number of years. As a result, the playwright's work is in some sense recognized as exemplary – yet paradoxically, it is precisely in being exemplary
that, as Attridge's comments imply, in the very act of challenging our
critical expectations, such 'acts of creativity' also resist generalization.
Frustratingly, in the course of provoking thought and in making us think,

this also ensures that literary texts are phantoms which finally resist critical appropriation. For how can we 'know' that which simultaneously remains beyond our full comprehension? Or even (as Marcellus requires of the scholar Horatio) 'speak to it'?

II Shakespeare after theory?

In seeking a definitive answer to that question, the draw of Shakespeare's texts has proved irresistible for many critics. Indeed, as the Shakespearean scholar Gary Taylor observes, it is as if the dramatist's corpus operates as the equivalent of an all-encompassing literary black hole:

> Light, insight, intelligence, matter – all pour ceaselessly into him, as critics are drawn into the densening vortex of his reputation; they add their own weight to his increasing mass . . . We find in Shakespeare only what we bring to him or what others have left behind; he gives us back our own values. And it is no use pretending that some uniquely clever, honest, and disciplined critic can find a technique, an angle, that will enable us to lead a mass escape from this trap. If Shakespeare is a literary black hole, then nothing that I, or anyone else, can say will make any difference. His accreting disk will go on spinning, sucking, growing . . .
>
> (Taylor 1990: 410–11)

In attempting to plug what, as Taylor implies, is an unpluggable abyss, even in this its imploded form, the metaphysical baggage which we relentlessly invest in the Bard has proved almost impossible to budge. Notwithstanding the uncertainties of interpretation I've outlined above, it follows that our predominant relation to the playwright's work is, as Taylor suggests, to foist our values upon him. As a result, petitions to Shakespeare still serve to legitimate a model for truth telling in contemporary culture. And this of course is no small part of the problem, tempting claims that are at once vague and unsituated, but also overweeningly hubristic in their assurance of somehow having grasped the total significance of the playwright's work. For all its wit and verve Harold Bloom's recent eulogy of *Shakespeare: The Invention of the Human* (1999) is, by its own admission, nothing more or less than a work of triumphal bardolatry. For Bloom, Shakespeare's uniqueness effectively underpins a secular religion, or as the critic himself puts it: 'He [Shakespeare] has become the first universal author, replacing the Bible in the secularized consciousness. Attempts to historicize his ascendancy continue to founder upon the uniqueness of his eminence' (Bloom 1999: 10). In a recent endorsement of Shakespeare as a 'Millennium Masterwork', Stanley

Wells offers a more Protestant account of what sounds like the same process:

> the works mirror the growth of a single human mind, that enable us to think of Shakespeare not just as a series of individual works but as a single Masterwork, a revelation of one man's response to the world around him, to his inheritance from the past and to the 'form and pressure' of the present.
>
> (Wells 1999: 14)

The emergence of literary theory over the past twenty years or so has gone some way towards unsettling the *gravitas* of these claims, and has helped expose them for the prescriptive forms of absolutism that they actually are. No end of political, feminist and historicist critiques of Shakespeare have served to remind us that literary 'truths', and the oppressive forms of identity which they police, are actually historically arbitrary and potentially renegotiable. Yet for many, Wells's assertion that Shakespeare's plays 'tell stories in ways that reach deep into the wells [*sic*] of human consciousness' (Wells 1999: 14) still rings true, and is met with barely a flicker. Indeed, if one is to judge anything by the sales of Bloom's book, we would do well to remember that Bloom the Yale professor and Wells the former director of the Shakespeare Institute hold the views which still predominate, and which, in their widespread dissemination, continue to maintain a significant foothold within what remains of the public sphere.

Where old-style literary criticism has tended to consolidate Shakespeare's reputation the impact of theory has tended to relativize it, and during what became known as the 'culture wars' of the late 1980s and early 1990s such 'hooligan' assaults on Shakespeare's authority were met with hostile opposition.[5] Yet for many critics, on the left as well as on the right, with the benefit of hindsight, the rhetoric of radical theory also often promised more than it actually delivered. Worse still, its 'relativist outlook' sometimes conceded too much to a form of postmodern scepticism which, in its turn away from Enlightenment values like 'truth', 'reason' and 'critique', threatened to leave us with a critical approach 'devoid of argumentative force' (Norris 1994: *passim*). While these issues are often misrepresentatively distorted in the public realm they also continue to stir debate amongst academics and media pundits alike. In a recent typical broadside from *The Sunday Times* the British philosopher Roger Scruton complains that the advance of theory actually represents an insidious dilution of critical thought:

> 'Deconstruction', 'différance' [*sic*], 'gender' – these are terms used to create an aura of thought in the absence of thought, and turn out, on

examination, to mean next to nothing . . . In the new university culture, non-thought competes on equal terms with thought . . . The fact is that debate and rational argument no longer have a central place in the world of the young, and not only because the soundbite culture has pushed them aside. Children are taught from an early age not to judge between opinions – to be 'sensitive' towards other cultures and other ways of thinking. If all options are equally valid, then none of them really matters – such is the inevitable conclusion of the multicultural and inclusive curriculum.

Students brought up in that way find it very difficult, when they enter university, to mean what they write in their weekly essays. How exactly can you mean 'Shakespeare understands the human heart', or 'Economic determinism is false', while knowing that someone is entitled to think the opposite?

(Scruton 1999: 11)

It is easy enough to dismiss this as a provocative rant, although even while Scruton might well be playing devil's advocate here, there is a chilling complacency surrounding his casual elimination of complex questions concerning cultural difference, and if nothing else, the philosopher's intervention offers us fairly cogent evidence that, in their 'openness' to dispute, the 'reasoned' arguments of liberal humanism are often nakedly complicit with the very totalitarian hierarchies they claim to oppose. Yet in a backhanded fashion, Scruton's defence of what he labels 'rational argument' also merits some further consideration.

Of course the problem with Scruton's invective (and this could be said to be true of the 'culture wars' more generally) is that it tends to polarize opinion between two rather reductive options. Either we must accept that Shakespeare's 'meaningfulness' is somehow ultimately testable or provable in the form Scruton suggests, or we must concede his argument that 'multiculturalism' is symptomatic of a type of unsituated free-for-all which abandons the question of valid distinctions altogether. Of course, the resultant caricature actually represents a travesty of literary theory, which, in opposing precisely the types of idealist prescriptions invoked by Scruton – 'Shakespeare understands the human heart' and so on – actually refuses to accept the imposition of normative categories without interrogating them first. Indeed, the significance of terms like 'gender', about which Scruton complains so vociferously, is that rather than constituting 'non-thought', they offer a far richer understanding of the implications of 'distinctions' of meaning than the philosopher can possibly muster – other, that is, than the unthinking platitude of intuition which he shorthands as Shakespeare's understanding 'of the human heart'. Ironically of course, in this respect, in its willingness to remain wary of traditional categories of evaluation, literary theory actually has a good deal more in common with the spirit of an Enlightenment project of emancipatory thought than Scruton would care to admit. While remaining equally concerned with the moral shortfall of the 'out-and-out cognitive scepticism' that certain strands of post-structuralist theory admittedly promote, Christopher Norris provides a far more thoughtful adjudication of the relativist slant of recent literary and cultural criticism, as he observes that:

> one could argue that just about every school of present-day critical thought, from deconstruction to New Historicism, acknowledges its debt – whether wittingly or not – to the legacy of Enlightenment critique. It is a project carried on in the deconstructive questioning of 'logocentric' values and truth-claims, in the effort to redeem those marginalised voices that have suffered the violence of colonial rule or the enormous condescension of posterity, and also – despite his anti-enlightenment rhetoric – in Foucault's genealogies of power/knowledge.
>
> That is to say, these thinkers take for granted a whole range of crucial distinctions – as between truth and falsehood, reason and rhetoric, real human interests and their distorted (ideological) representation – which no amount of *de rigueur* postmodern scepticism can entirely conceal from view. Such projects would lack any meaning or purpose (would indeed be quite unintelligible) were it not for their tacitly acknowledged commitment to those same principles and values . . . For the very terms in which their arguments are couched – historical, sociological, ethico-political – are terms that quite literally *make no sense* if removed from the validating context of enlightened thought.
>
> (Norris 1994: 32–3)

In directing theory back to 'the legacy of Enlightenment critique' of which it is part, Norris also indirectly opens the way to a more reflective engagement with the very philosophical precursors which, in the first instance, provided a condition of possibility for the eventual emergence of literary theory itself. The tradition of reflective critique to which he refers us arguably locates one of its most significant inaugural moments in Kant's essay of 1784 'An answer to the question: what is enlightenment', where the philosopher coins his 'motto of enlightenment', that is 'Sapere Aude! "Have courage to use your own understanding!" ' (Kant 1983: 41). I should hasten to add that Kant's declaration of an independent thinking self is *not* to be confused with the plenitudinous wellspring of 'human consciousness' promulgated by Stanley Wells and his ilk. Living with the consequence of a 'self-validating' rational autonomy does not represent an 'acquiescence' to some notion of an unchanging organic human identity. Rather, an enlightened critique of 'dogmatic metaphysics' effectively implies a radical actualization of the self, which locates cognitive scepticism in its more critical context, and in doing so indirectly affirms the 'essential historicity' of the 'knowing' subject. In the process the 'self' is effectively dislocated, in terms which relativize the tradition of thought itself. Simon Critchley provides a helpful gloss on the experience:

> One might say that the gain of the Continental tradition [post-Kant] is that it allows one to focus on the essential historicity of philosophy as a practice and the essential historicity of the philosopher who engages in this practice ... the recognition of the essential historicity of philosophy (and philosophers) implies: (i) the radical *finitude* of the human subject, i.e. that there is no God-like standpoint or point of reference outside of human experience from which the latter might be characterized and judged; and (ii) the thoroughly *contingent* or *created* character of human experience.
>
> (Critchley 1998: 10)[6]

Of course, in unravelling the consequence of 'the contingent and created character of human experience' to which Critchley refers, in its earliest forms, the radical Shakespearean criticism of the 1980s was quick enough to locate the 'invention of the human' as the unstable fiction that it actually is. And one need only glimpse at ground-breaking texts of Renaissance criticism such as Jonathan Dollimore's *Radical Tragedy* (1984), Catherine Belsey's *The Subject of Tragedy* (1985), Stephen Greenblatt's *Renaissance Self-fashioning* (1980) and Francis Barker's *The Tremulous Private Body* (1984) to see that, in the course of questioning its own conditions of emergence, from its early modern inception onwards, the 'self' has 'trembled' on the point of its collapse. In unleashing desires and appetites which would exceed reason and move beyond its confines, as Hugh Grady has recently reminded us (Grady 1996), Shakespeare's world is very much of the world of Machiavelli and Nietzsche. Even Harold Bloom would concede this much, and one need look no further than the character of Edmund in *King Lear* to locate the destructive consequence of an early modern subject unshackled from the constraints of tradition. Yet the problem, as Grady himself suggests in Chapter 3, is that even while literary theory remained fully aware of the transgressive impulse of overcoming the self, it did not weigh the consequence of this event reflectively enough. In critiquing the conditions of modern subjectivity and opposing the inscription of the self 'as an object of rational knowledge' (cf. e.g. Barker 1984), cultural materialism and new historicism tended to place an emphasis on the negation of the self, without conceding that, as Critchley and Dews recently put it, in the complex history of its emergence, the subject 'may appear, in many of its guises, to be the one of the driving forces *behind* – rather than the prime defence against . . . [an] unravelling of metaphysics' (Critchley and Dews 1996: 1, my emphasis).

Stanley Cavell's early seminal re-evaluation of the philosophical significance of Shakespeare's plays (which emerged at the same moment as cultural materialism and new historicism but, initially at least, seemed to be removed from their concerns) serves to remind us just how complex this sceptical 'unravelling' can be. For Cavell, Othello's doomed desire to validate Desdemona's affection beyond all reasonable doubt remains an exemplary instance of a 'desire for certainty' in the playwright's work which can be exposed as a rage at the non-identity of the other (Cavell 1987: cf. 125–42). In Cavell's account, it is precisely because scepticism is forced to concede the limits of experience beyond its grasp that it exposes us to the possibility that we might 'acknowledge' the 'otherness of the human'.[7] In the course of relocating our understanding of scepticism in what is now in some sense its 'post-theoretical' context, the Shakespearean trajectory of Cavell's work ushers in an ethical response which is not wholly out of sync with the work of philosophers like Levinas and Derrida. It is difficult to see how a criticism which claims to be 'political' could ignore this call to justice. Indeed, in Derrida's recent reading of Marx it is none other than the spirit of Hamlet who exemplifies a non-foundationalist petition to justice which remains unfulfilled (cf. Derrida 1994), though so far the implications of this aspect of Derrida's work have gone largely unremarked in radical currents of Shakespeare criticism.

In beginning to develop the implications of Cavell's work for a materialist criticism, we might say that if Shakespeare's texts *are* philosophical dramas, then it is because they retain an ethical dimension without transcending those social, historical and linguistic limitations, which simultaneously remain in need of redress, and actually conjure an ethical situation into being. In contrast of course, the problem with more traditional and absolutist accounts of the 'moral stature' of the playwright's work, offered by critics like Bloom, Wells, Scruton and the like, is that they tend to the opposite, in reverting to the transcendentalist imperative which would remove Shakespeare from our world altogether, and thereby, in the same process, eliminate the potential for an effective critique. It follows that for critics like Bloom, Shakespeare is finally qualitatively different *only* because he 'overcomes all demarcations between cultures, or within culture' (Bloom 1999: 11).

Despite its protestation of all-encompassing breadth, in keeping with most narrow understandings of Western rationalism, liberal humanism exhibits an idealist tendency to assume that 'knowledge forms a single system' (cf. Speake 1979: 298–9). Yet the distinctive *value* of Shakespeare remains that, as A. D. Nuttall recently put it: 'His [Shakespeare's] writing has the effect of making all other thought appear coarsely schematic' (Nuttall 1999: 133–4). In an important sense, the creative or literary dimension to which I referred earlier clearly holds the key here. Indeed, we could say that the very impossibility of imposing a final or unified meaning upon the plays *is* what makes them literature (cf. Bowie 1997). And paradoxically of course, the 'interpretative ambiguity' which the playwright's work engenders (what Emerson terms Shakespeare's 'inconceivability') also in turn ensures his potential value to philosophy, confirming a relation which the philosopher David Wood elaborates in the following terms:

> While literature may not allow us to adjudicate on philosophical claims, there is every reason to think that the possibilities of imaginative description offered by literature can help us to grasp what, in practice, certain philosophical claims might come to. If literature is or can be something of an experimental exploration of the ramifications of a philosophical position, and if that process is an essential dimension to the consideration one gives to a philosophical claim, then a philosophy that did not have its literary enactments or corollaries would be radically deficient.
>
> (Wood 1990: 2)

Rather than regarding Shakespeare as a poor unwitting adjunct of reason or as somehow subsumed within its project, the dramatist's open-ended resistance to conceptual control might finally turn out to be a far more crucial resource for critical thought. In this sense, we might say that Shakespeare unwittingly provides access to the 'literary conditions of philosophical questioning' itself.[8] And in these circumstances, as Andrew Bowie observes: 'The need to integrate the disciplines of literary study and philosophy in new ways is vital to the longer-term health of both disciplines' (Bowie 1997: 2).

III Philosophical Shakespeares

In considering Shakespeare in relation to individual thinkers or certain intellectual traditions, in different forms, the chapters in this book explore various strands in the developing dialogue between philosophy and literature to which Bowie refers.

The volume opens with Michael Bristol's interrogation of meaning and motivation in *Macbeth*, in response to the provocation offered by L. C.

Knights' critical classic 'How many children had Lady Macbeth?' (1946). In a sharply focused and provocative analysis, Bristol suggests that we need to reconsider how far our understanding of Shakespeare's plays is necessarily co-ordinated with our knowledge of everyday life. As Bristol demonstrates, such an approach need not mark a retreat into uncritical literal-mindedness. Considering the status of 'truth in fiction' in relation to recent debates within analytical philosophy, his chapter pilots a reading of the play which situates the 'possible worlds' of make-believe as the complex forms of social interaction that they actually are.

In Chapter 3, 'On the need for a differentiated theory of (early) modern subjects', Hugh Grady returns us to the contemporary context of Shakespeare criticism. Grady argues that the tendency of materialist criticism to make use of umbrella or composite terms like 'liberal humanism' produces an understanding of subjectivity which is misleadingly one-dimensional and reductively over-functionalist. In providing an incisive critique of Renaissance criticism's early theorization of the production of the self within modernity, Grady explores the possibilities for a more complex genealogy of early modern subjectivity. Turning instead to theorists of the Frankfurt School of the first and second generation, he urges us to 'think subjectivity' in forms which remain open to the critical, creative and transfigurative potentialities of selfhood, as well as, or in addition to, its construction within a realm of ideology and power.

In extending the thesis of Bruno Latour's *We Have Never Been Modern* (1993), Linda Charnes sidesteps the opposition between modernity and postmodernity altogether, as she situates Shakespeare's *Hamlet* and Gus Van Sant's 'recasting' of the *Henriad* in the film *My Own Private Idaho* (1992) as proliferating unrecountable and temporally complex 'non-modern' hybrids, which do not fit comfortably into more conventional epistemological categories. Along with Scott Wilson's chapter, Charnes's contribution locates us at the very limits of contemporary disenchantment where, in the popular imaginary of a culture 'actively enervating disbelief', the 'affective' historicity of an increasingly apparitional Shakespeare now effectively substitutes for 'History itself'.

David Johnson (Chapter 5) returns us to a more traditional account of the historical settlement of what Charnes provocatively shorthands as philosophy's 'modern Constitution', by reminding us of the oppressive legacy of European thought in its colonial context. As Johnson suggests, a 'Philosophical Shakespeare' is bound at best to retain a restrictively Eurocentric inflection, and at worst to highlight the substantial involvement of philosophy in legitimating the process of imperialism itself. His chapter interrogates the formative relation between German and English constructions of Shakespeare and nationhood set out during the Romantic and Victorian periods, and pays particular attention to the assimilation of these ideas within the emergent public sphere of the Cape Colony. In the course of exploring the relation between the aesthetic and the nation theorized by A. W. Schlegel's *Course of Lectures on Dramatic Art and Literature* (1846) and the contemporaneous Shakespeare criticism of Archdeacon Nathaniel Merriman, Johnson convincingly demonstrates that the fragility of the European Shakespeares constituted in the Romantic period is all too evident in the anxious versions of metropolitan criticism produced by early colonial literati.

The threat of meaninglessness could be construed as another symptom of philosophy's taking the claim of Shakespeare's relation to truth and domination seriously. But, in Shakespeare, nihilism also appears in a surprising variety of guises, and in each of the two chapters which draw the volume to a close, it transpires that the playwright's work discloses the potential to accommodate a range of equivocal registers for the negation or transvaluation of meaning. In a detailed elaboration of a fragment from *Ecce Homo*, Scott Wilson (Chapter 6) looks at the importance to Nietzsche of Shakespeare, particularly his genealogy of morals and his notion of the will to power. As Wilson suggests, the location of Shakespeare in Nietzsche is an extremely complex and contradictory one. Yet, to read Nietzsche reading Shakespeare is to read 'Shakespeare with intensity', newly attending to the heterogeneous and in some sense inexpressible moments that litter the playwright's texts and which in their apprehension of difference affirm a 'lofty morality' which overcomes any settled notion of good and evil. In a reading which develops the implications of Nietzsche's notion of 'impulsive intensity' across a range of political, theatrical and cultural contexts, Wilson presents us with a 'thinker' willing to think beyond the moral rationalizations of a 'modern' discourse of political emancipation.

Thinking beyond conventional philosophical categories is also a feature of Howard Caygill's chapter. In contemplating 'Shakespeare's monster of nothing', Caygill effectively demonstrates that in his 'stagings of nothing', the playwright produces a richness of thought about nothing and its relations with the King, the thing and the many. These diverse phrasings of 'nothing' are read alongside the philosophical stagings of nothing in the work of Hegel and Heidegger. Caygill argues that the preoccupation of philosophical phrasings of nihilism, with the reduction to nothing through the negation of the thing, leads to a narrow understanding of nihilism. By way of contrast, in place of Heidegger's ontological 'Why is there something rather than nothing', Caygill intriguingly suggests that Shakespeare's stagings evoke the question 'Why is there not nothing rather than nothing'. Caygill argues that nothing here can be staged in terms not only of negation, but also *as* absence and reduction to zero, modes of nihilism less frequently proposed in philosophical texts.

IV Last words?

> Adieu, adieu, adieu. Remember me.
>
> (*Hamlet* I. v. 91)

Viewed in hindsight, it is striking just how many of the chapters briefly sampled above redeploy Shakespearean texts and characters in terms which demand redemption, but only in forms which simultaneously refuse redress: Lady Macbeth's 'missing' children, the waning affectivity of Shakespeare's claim to historicity, the Shakespearean stagings of 'not-nothing' explored by Howard Caygill and, most ubiquitous of all of course, the spectre of Hamlet who, as well as featuring in at least two of the chapters, already stalks the very margins of the book itself. Perhaps this is merely to observe that, while there is evidently still a great deal at stake in metaphysical questions, these days we tend to frame our enquiries more cautiously.

Yet, ironically of course, in the face of such uncertainties the quest for the ontological certainty of 'Shakespeare' remains almost fully intact. Most recently, even the relatively arcane question of whether or not Shakespeare was (or is?) a Catholic served to stir considerable media controversy, wholly out of kilter with its actual empirical significance. At their best such conjectures are thought-provoking and illuminate new contexts for our understanding of the plays, though at their worst they shelter under the rainbow alliance of the type of nostalgic antiquarianism which continues to vie over the relative merits of the Earl of Oxford or Sir Francis Bacon as the true sovereign source of the playwright's work. Bardolatry of course draws its water from the same well, and the extraordinary impact of Harold Bloom's book is no doubt indirectly symptomatic of a *fin-de-millennium* malaise which, in the midst of its wider perception that modern culture is increasingly devoid of value, against all the odds somehow desperately wants to preserve a sense of the meaningfulness of the playwright's work.

In this respect of course, for Harold Bloom, a belief in Shakespeare's survival is in no small part synonymous with his contemporaneity, indeed in some sense the playwright is more modern than we are:

> Bardolatry, the worship of Shakespeare, ought to be a more secular religion than it already is. The plays remain the outward limit of human achievement: aesthetically, cognitively, in certain ways morally, even spiritually. They abide beyond the end of the mind's reach; we cannot catch up to them. Shakespeare will go on explaining us, in part because he invented us.
>
> (Bloom 1999: xvii–xviii)

While the critic seems to lay his cards clearly on the table here, on closer inspection, in couching his introductory remarks on Shakespeare's infinite transcendence in terms of 'Bardolatry' or 'secular religion', Bloom actually pulls off what is in effect a disingenuous double take, so that, as Donald Lyons observes, in his broader defence of the Bard as secular scripture:

> He [Bloom] insists again and again on the absence of religious belief – of Christian context – behind the plays. Then, having taken God out of Shakespeare, he proceeds to erect the playwright and his work into curious objects of worship.
>
> (Lyons 1999: 54)

Paradoxically of course, whatever Bloom means by casting Shakespeare as a 'mortal god', historically speaking at least, the modern-day mythologization of the playwright as a secular icon actually locates its most important formative context during the post-Restoration assimilation of Shakespeare within the rationalizing processes of the modern public sphere (cf. Dobson 1992, de Grazia 1991, Taylor 1990). As such, the onset of 'Bardolatry' coincides directly with the emergence of philosophical scepticism and the rejection of myth and religious belief in favour of reason (cf. Speake 1979: 299). In short, disenchantment only ever serves to usher in new forms of re-enchantment as its necessary accomplice. And while Bloom occludes this process by completely failing to pin down the notion of Bardolatry in anything like its historical context, there is actually an extremely complex resonance to be remarked here, between the contemporary 'post-metaphysical' collapse of our own belief systems and the inauguration of philosophical modernity itself. Indeed, in one form, as Peter Dews puts it, then as now: 'Just as the end of myth can itself only be recounted as myth . . . the story of the end of metaphysics will itself always open on to a metaphysical dimension' (Dews 1995: 13). In its own way, if Bardolatry is still alive and well in a secular world, this no doubt indirectly testifies to the fact that (to reappropriate Dews's provocative phrase for the process) there are still 'limits to our disenchantment'. Yet this need not necessitate an uncritical return to a new essentialism, nor should it be to insist with Bloom that we must 'worship in a secular way'.

The late modern predicament of disenchantment to which Dews alludes manifests itself in a variety of forms in contemporary culture and perhaps we should not be surprised that Shakespeare is at the hub of it. In the face of a pragmatic elimination of a distinction between literature and philosophy, the semantic indeterminacies and ontological ambiguities of the playwright's work still somehow remain indispensable to us in making a difference. No doubt, this is partly because, in their own way, the question(s) of how we remember, of disenchantment and re-enchantment, of presence and non-presence, being and not being, knowing and not knowing, are themselves necessarily linked in intricate ways to the literary critical 'event' of re-reading itself. Indeed, in some sense, as Stephen Greenblatt reminds us, our negotiation of old Hamlet's death is an exemplary case in point, insofar as it effectively constitutes the singular act of witness or memorial, which will continue to assure and maintain our literary critical life – 'Thou art a scholar, speak to it, Horatio . . .' (Greenblatt 1997: 481).

For my own part, without confusing remembering with monumentalism as Bloom tends to,[9] I am happy to concede that Shakespeare remains as modern as we are. Yet, crucially, this is *not* merely to label the playwright our latter-day contemporary. Indeed, insofar as the plays appear to anticipate our discontents then, for Shakespearean scholars and philosophers alike, the interpretative validity of the plays will continue to remain non-reducible to a linear account of history. In the midst of theorizing Shakespeare in the mid-1980s, Terry Eagleton inadvertently confirms a still more complex sense of what it might mean to negotiate Shakespeare philosophically:

> Those who are sceptical of the relevance of contemporary critical theory to the Swan of Avon should remember that there are more anachronisms in Shakespeare's plays than the clock in *Julius Caesar*. Though conclusive evidence is hard to come by, it is difficult to read Shakespeare without feeling that he was almost certainly familiar with the writings of Hegel, Marx, Nietzsche, Freud, Wittgenstein and Derrida. Perhaps this is simply to say that though there are many ways in which we have thankfully left this conservative patriarch behind, there are other ways in which we have yet to catch up with him.
>
> (Eagleton 1986: ix–x)

On a superficial reading Eagleton's observation might appear to vindicate the Bloomsian sentiment that Shakespeare 'is still out ahead of us'. Yet, in effect, his observation echoes Hans-Georg Gadamer, or indeed Walter Benjamin, in suggesting that 'works of art might yet come to know their moment'. Historically speaking, as Eagleton's comments testify, the relationship between literature and its criticism is very much a two-way street, and insofar as we continue to appropriate Shakespeare, it's worth remembering that Shakespeare also continues to appropriate us.[10] Viewed in its post-theoretical context, the fuller purchase of 're-reading' Shakespeare might be said to lie in developing a more rigorous understanding of the necessary hermeneutical entwinement of philosophy and literature that Eagleton's remarks serve to insinuate. In this sense, the process of re-reading Shakespeare is not part of some universal or 'never ending' process; indeed, in some respects, it can only ever be said to have just begun.

Notes

1 For a penetrating reconceptualization of the significance of these traditions for contemporary literary theory, see Bowie 1997.
2 For more on the literary milieu in question and the emergence within it of notions concerning Shakespeare's 'original genius', see Bate 1992 and Bate 1997: 157–86.
3 I'm grateful to William Kerrigan for drawing my attention to Emerson's observation, cf. Kerrigan 1998: 30–1.
4 I'm indebted to Derek Attridge 1999 for this distinction.
5 For a representative sampling of these skirmishes, see Kamps 1991.
6 Thanks to Simon Critchley 1998 for clarifying several of the distinctions made above concerning the critical confrontation of philosophy with its own tradition.
7 This reading of Cavell draws directly from Gerald Bruns's work: see Bruns 1990: 612–32, cf. esp. 614–17.
8 Again a project wholly aligned with Cavell's ground-breaking work on Shakespeare. I'm grateful to Timothy Gould 1992 for this formulation and for illuminating this aspect of Cavell's work, cf. esp. p. 64.
9 For a fuller critique of Bloom's 'monumentalising gesture' and for an exemplary interrogation of the question of monumentalism and literary value in its Shakespearean context, see Bennett and Royle 1999: 44–53.
10 Though this is not merely to say, as Bloom does, that: 'the plays read me better than I read them' (Bloom 1999: xx).

2
How many children did she have?
MICHAEL D. BRISTOL

I have a guilty secret: I want to know how many children Lady Macbeth had. I have a further admission to make. When I read Shakespeare I compare the dramatic characters with real people. I do not make such admissions lightly. 'How many children had Lady Macbeth?' is a byword for asinine literal-mindedness, as if asking a question about a literary character's children is something that would never occur to minimally competent readers. But what's wrong with wanting to know how many children Lady Macbeth had anyway? 'Even stupid questions have answers' as Linus once remarked to Lucy. It's not, after all, like asking what Duncan's blood type was, or whether Banquo ever had the measles. Lady Macbeth makes explicit reference to her experience of motherhood. Children are thematically important to the play's structure. Finally, there is the question of Macbeth's heirs. It seems entirely reasonable to raise questions about the Macbeth children, even if Shakespeare's play does not provide any satisfactory answers.

Romeo and Juliet are teenagers who fall in love. Hamlet can't make up his mind. King Lear is like my father-in-law. Intuitions like this are routinely dismissed by professional critics as naive. But as a matter of fact King Lear *is* like my father-in-law: they both have three daughters, they both own real estate, and each has been known to behave unreasonably. All things considered, however, it would be better not to pursue such reflections, not only for the sake of my professional reputation, but also for the sake of peace in the family. Though, while the habit of thinking about literary characters as comparable to the people who actually populate one's own life may be unwise, it is also extremely persistent outside the institutions of academic criticism.

Just how did Helena and Diana get away with the bed trick? Where was Hamlet when his father was killed? What happened to Lady Macbeth's baby? This is naive in a somewhat different way from thinking that my father-in-law is like King Lear. The problem here is not that the interpretation refers unthinkingly to one's own existential situation. The difficulty is the contrasting one of sticking your head through the frame and trying to see what else is in the picture. The text of *Othello* doesn't really say whether the sexual relationship of Othello and Desdemona was unusually passionate or conventionally chaste, or whether they had no sexual relationship at all, as some commentators maintain. And furthermore, no one has any business trying to find out. The story is just what the text says it is, no more, no less. Serious readers should concentrate on the verbal composition instead of wasting time speculating about what might have happened during gaps in the narrative.

It is easy for professional scholars to say what is wrong-headed in vernacular interpretations of Shakespeare. What is more difficult to grasp is why interpretative practices of this kind seem obvious and sensible ways to respond to the plays. This chapter will not reiterate the rudimentary insight that persons are not texts or vice versa. I intend to pursue the opposing claim that it is reasonable to think about literary characters the way we think about real people because that is how we actually make sense of stories. When someone compares their ageing parent to King Lear, or wonders what happened to Lady Macbeth's child, their interest reflects a sophisticated grasp of how fiction is co-ordinated with our knowledge of everyday life.

In the first section of this chapter I look very specifically at the question of Lady Macbeth's children. This topic is addressed by way of a reconsideration of two much earlier discussions of the play. I begin with A. C. Bradley's 'notes' on *Macbeth*, which constitute a series of afterthoughts to his lectures on the play in *Shakespearean Tragedy* (1992). This is followed with a discussion of L. C. Knights' influential article, 'How many children had Lady Macbeth?' Bradley's interest in such questions as when Macbeth first plotted to kill Duncan is much closer to vernacular interpretation than the close textual scrutiny advocated by Knights. In the second section of the chapter I propose a theoretical model for understanding how readers get what's going on in a complex story like *Macbeth*. This model is based primarily on recent work on the practice of make-believe by Kendall Walton, David Lewis and Gregory Currie. This work can be extremely helpful in showing exactly what ordinary readers do when they participate in the institution of making-believe. Approaching Shakespeare's plays by way of the attitude of make-believe won't reveal what happened to Lady Macbeth's child. But it can help show what interests motivate this question and why it is important.

I Lady Macbeth and her children

Well, how many children *did* Lady Macbeth have? The question is not completely adventitious. At the very beginning of the play, Lady Macbeth makes explicit and quite vivid reference not only to the existence of a child, but to the very intimate experience of breast-feeding:

> What beast was't then,
> That made you break this enterprise to me?
> When you durst do it, then you were a man;
> And, to be more than what you were, you would
> Be so much more the man. Nor time, nor place,
> Did then adhere, and yet you would make both:
> They have made themselves, and that their fitness now
> Does unmake you. I have given suck, and know
> How tender 't is to love the babe that milks me:
> I would, while it was smiling in my face,
> Have pluck'd my nipple from his boneless gums,
> And dash'd the brains out, had I so sworn
> As you have done to this.
>
> (I. vii. 47–59)

A. C. Bradley considers this passage in a note about when Duncan's murder was first plotted. Bradley is preoccupied with Macbeth's 'guilty ambition' and in particular with figuring out when the thought of murdering Duncan was first conceived. The point of Bradley's analysis is that a firm plan to kill Duncan had already been considered by Macbeth before he ever heard the witches' prophecy. Lady Macbeth reminds her husband that he initially proposed the murder at some earlier point, but that 'he did so at a time when there was no opportunity to attack Duncan' (Bradley 1992: 455). Macbeth has sworn to create such an occasion and Lady Macbeth advises him that he will never have a better chance to carry out his plan.

Bradley views this passage as what is known as 'back story' – events that have occurred prior to the opening of *Macbeth*. The reference helps to supply information about the motives and intentions of the characters. Bradley's point is important, since it establishes premeditation on the part of Macbeth. Duncan's murder is not a rash impulse, nor is it prompted either by the witches' prophecy or by Lady Macbeth. Bradley is at some pains to establish forethought and cold calculation on the part of Macbeth. But although he quotes Lady Macbeth's speech in its entirety, he does not comment specifically on the gruesome reference to the killing of a beloved infant. If the point here is to understand the implications of 'back story', then why doesn't Lady Macbeth's reference to a baby carry more weight? The existence of a baby is relevant to questions of motive, especially since the reference to '*his* boneless gums' reveals that this baby is a boy and therefore Macbeth's presumptive heir.

In a subsequent note, Bradley takes up the question of Macbeth's heirs more directly. He begins by noting the soliloquy in III. i. where Macbeth ruminates on the witches' prophecy:

> then, prophet-like,
> They hail'd him father to a line of kings:
> Upon my head they plac'd a fruitless crown,
> And put a barren sceptre in my gripe,
> Thence to be wrench'd with an unlineal hand,
> No son of mine succeeding.
>
> (III. i. 58–63)

This could imply that Macbeth has many sons, or that he has none. Bradley thinks it suggests pretty clearly that Macbeth 'looked forward to having [a son]' (Bradley 1992: 464). But later, when Macduff has been told that his 'wife and babes' have been slaughtered, he seems to suggest that Macbeth has no heirs:

> He has no children. – All my pretty ones?
> Did you say all? – O hell-kite! – All?
> What, all my pretty chickens, and their dam,
> At one fell swoop?
>
> (IV. iii. 216–19)

Bradley wants to determine whether Macduff is referring here to Malcolm or to Macbeth. He concludes that, of several interpretations, the most satisfactory is that the lines 'refer to Macbeth, who has no children, and on whom therefore Macduff cannot take an adequate revenge' (Bradley 1992: 466).

Just for the record, Bradley never spends time fussing about how *many* children Lady Macbeth had. He takes it as given that she has had a child, based on the lines already quoted. But he also states that: 'Whether Macbeth had children or (as seems usually to be supposed) had none, is quite immaterial' (464). Bradley's analysis seems to overlook a rather puzzling fact about the story. If Macbeth 'has no children' then what happened to the baby Lady Macbeth so lovingly nursed, and then was so ready to sacrifice? There are several plausible answers to this question. The most obvious explanation is that the infant Lady Macbeth suckled has since died, which might account for Macbeth's reference to 'a rooted sorrow' in the brain (V. iii. 41–2) as a possible explanation for her madness. Another alternative is that Lady Macbeth has a child, but Macbeth is not the father. This would be possible if Lady Macbeth were a widow and Macbeth were her second husband. Bradley insists that Shakespeare's text provides no way to determine the fate of Lady Macbeth's child: 'We cannot say, and it does not concern the play' (465). His primary concern, however, is to use the author's text as a resource for understanding the story the author intends to tell. He therefore treats individual speeches as sources of information about what characters have done or what they contemplate doing. When Lady Macbeth tells her husband: 'I have given suck, and know / How tender 't is to love the babe that milks me' (I. vii. 54–5), Bradley views her words as the expression of her 'strained exaltation'. But it never occurs to him to doubt the existence of an actual baby as the source for this emotion.

Bradley's close attention to textual detail proceeds from his background assumptions about the way a text can represent what people are capable of doing: 'We see a number of human beings placed in certain circumstances; and we see, arising from the co-operation of their characters in these circumstances, certain actions' (6). Bradley thinks that people have reasons for what they say and do. He also assumes that his background knowledge about how people ordinarily interact with each other is useful as a way to understand what is happening in a literary work. On this view the same reasons that determine the actions of our friends, neighbours and business associates can also be discovered in the actions of Shakespeare's tragic heroes (see Brown in Bradley 1992: xiii). When people speak, their utterances reflect not only their own beliefs and attitudes, but also their beliefs about the beliefs and attitudes of whoever it is they are talking to. So, for example, when a woman tells her husband she knows what it is to nurse an infant it seems likely this is a reference to a child rather than a rhetorical flourish.

The decisive interdiction of Bradley's orientation comes with L. C. Knights' influential article 'How many children had Lady Macbeth?', first published in 1933. Knights' aim is to demonstrate how to study 'Shakespeare as a poet' (Knights 1946: 1). In order to address this task, he must first dispose of what he calls 'the most fruitful of irrelevancies', namely the 'assumption that Shakespeare was pre-eminently a great "creator of characters"' (p. 1). Knights acknowledges that A. C. Bradley provides the most 'illustrious example' of this approach and describes Bradley's achievement as one in which the 'detective interest supersedes the critical' (p. 3). Bradley's preoccupation with detection leads him 'to conjecture upon Hamlet's whereabouts at the time of his father's death' (p. 3). Somehow the reader grasps that this is a really stupid question, but Knights does not take time to explain exactly why Bradley's concern with character is incompatible with the basic standards of real criticism. He is convinced, however, that the study of character misses what is truly salient in the works of Elizabethan drama.

With the possible exception of Dr Johnson, eighteenth-century critics of Shakespeare suffered from the same 'inability to appreciate the Elizabethan idiom and a consequent inability to discuss Shakespeare's plays as poetry' (p. 13). Because they failed to recognize the 'indivisible unity of a Shakespeare play' these critics developed the bad habit of abstracting the characters from the literary text and treating them as if they were real people. Knights' critique does not indict character criticism for its complicity with an emerging bourgeois ideology. To the contrary, he views this preoccupation with ' "personality" in fiction' as the manifestation of Romanticism. In fairness to Knights it must be admitted that eighteenth- and nineteenth-century character criticism is often vague, rambling and sentimental. There are plenty of examples of critical ditherings about the beauty of nature or the tenderness of young love in nineteenth-century criticism. By the time Knights was working on his own essay, this tradition must have seemed completely vapid – a *langage de bois* completely tangential to the complex verbal artefacts created by Shakespeare: 'Wherever we look we find the same reluctance to master the words of the play, the same readiness to abstract a character and treat him (because he is more manageable that way) as a human being' (p. 15). Knights scarcely attempts to understand why such an error, if that's what it was, took hold, why it has persisted for so long, or why so many otherwise intelligent people thought it was an interesting and sensible way to talk about Shakespeare. He does not explain why the assumptions that might have guided William Richardson or Anna Jameson or A. C. Bradley are unreasonable. They are just wrong.

The real aim of 'How many children had Lady Macbeth?' is to make the case for studying Shakespeare's works as poetry rather than as something like a soap opera or a romantic novel, where attention to the vagaries of character might conceivably be appropriate. For Knights this means looking at these artefacts as purely verbal structures:

> We start with so many lines of verse on a printed page which we read as we should read any other poem. We have to elucidate the meaning (using Dr Richards's fourfold definition) and to unravel ambiguities; we

have to estimate the kind and quality of the imagery and determine the precise degree of evocation of particular figures; we have to allow full weight to each word, exploring its 'tentacular roots', and to determine how it controls and is controlled by the rhythmic movement of the passage in which it occurs.

(16)

Serious critics look at the text and not at what the text is talking about. In one form or another, this doctrine continues to be an important one for literary criticism. There are many contemporary critics who regard 'theory' as an 'orientation to language as such' (see Miller 1987 as cited in Mullaney 1996: 18). Knights does not advance the extravagant claim that there is nothing outside the text. He seems perfectly willing to concede that there are people, animals, physical objects and so forth that populate his world. Nor does he argue for indeterminacy of meaning, but rather for an over-determination of meaning within the formal boundaries of the literary work. But Knights does not actually explain why 'the text' should have this pre-eminence or how it is in fact possible to accomplish the trick of talking about the language of a Shakespeare play without noticing what the characters are doing.

Knights offers a detailed illustration of the right way to talk about a Shakespeare play as poetry: '*Macbeth* is a statement of evil' (p. 18). In a way Knights' critical demonstration is in trouble before it even gets off the ground. The argument is extraordinary in the way it attempts to adumbrate the notion of evil without any reference to human agency. A statement of evil, we are told 'is a statement not of a philosophy but of ordered emotion' (p. 29). Here again it is evident that ordered emotion can have a meaningful existence without reference to the mental states of any human agents. *Macbeth* interweaves 'reversal of values' with 'unnatural disorder' and then adds an element of 'deceitful appearance' (p. 18). It's by no means clear why a focus on abstract metaphysical topics represents a significant intellectual advance over the tradition of character criticism. Knights is very definite in claiming that he has worked out an effective way to talk about Shakespeare's works 'as poetry', but he doesn't really try to explain why this reorientation is important.

And what about Lady Macbeth's children? Knights absolutely refuses to talk about this question, even though it provides the title for the essay. Knights expounds Lady Macbeth's lines about murdering her own child as the elaboration of the general theme of 'unnatural' feelings. But why is it unnatural to feel like dashing out the brains of your own baby? The interpretation here obviously depends on a judgement about Lady Macbeth as a mother. Her intended behaviour is 'unnatural' only in relation to a normative inference that says mothers are supposed to love and protect their babies. So it appears that Knights has not really avoided talking about how many children Lady Macbeth had. But what is so frightening about the question of Lady Macbeth's children? Knights' deeper concern is not really with a larger principle of literary interpretation, but with an admonition that Lady Macbeth's child must not be talked about. The forbidden action is openly talking about the possibility that a woman might be willing to murder her own children in the interest of her ambition.

The thought of a mother deliberately killing her own baby is pretty frightening, though Shakespeare was clearly not afraid to invent a character who could contemplate such a deed. In his essay on 'Macbeth and witch-craft', Peter Stallybrass has argued that the existence of a narrative anomaly in the case of Lady Macbeth's children may have a symbolic justification:

> the notorious question, 'How many children had Lady Macbeth?' is not entirely irrelevant. For although Lady Macbeth says, 'I have given suck' (1. 7. 54), her children are never seen on the stage, unlike the children of Duncan, Banquo, Macduff, and Siward. Are we not asked to accept a logical contradiction for the sake of a symbolic unity: Lady Macbeth is *both* an unnatural mother *and* sterile? This links her to the unholy family of the Witches, with their familiars and their brew which includes 'Finger of birth-strangled babe' and the blood of a sow which has eaten its own litter (4. 1. 30 and 64–65). Like the Witches, Lady Macbeth and her husband constitute an 'unholy' family, a family whose only children are the 'murth'ring ministers'.
>
> (Stallybrass 1996: 111–12)

Stallybrass manages to capture what may be the really salient point in Knights' essay without threatening excommunication of anyone who shows an interest in literary characters. There is, of course, no logical contradiction involved in the fact that Lady Macbeth's children never appear on stage. But Stallybrass implies that this non-appearance is a structuring absence required for the identification of Lady Macbeth as a witch. The children don't appear because they don't exist (Lady Macbeth is a witch and therefore sterile) but she is willing to murder the infant she has nursed (Lady Macbeth is a bad mother). It's not just that there is not enough explicit textual support for any of the possible theories about how many children she had. The narrative contradiction is *required* in order to convey this figure's semantic and ideological payload.

The extreme version of a text-orientated position proposed by L. C. Knights does not simply rule out questions about Lady Macbeth's child on the grounds that the story is incomplete. The argument goes further and denies that we have a legitimate *interest* in pursuing the question at all. Stallybrass's essay represents a pragmatic compromise. Like Bradley, he accepts the text as a necessary constraint on what we actually know about the lives of characters. But he also sees that certain kinds of background knowledge contribute significantly to a competent grasp of any story. So the text can hold together, but only as a symbolic pattern, just as Knights insisted. The downside is that the story doesn't make sense. The proposition that Lady Macbeth has had a child is true (she nursed a baby) and also false (there are no heirs). In real life women either have babies or they don't have them. It begins to look as if L. C. Knights is right after all. There is a fundamental conceptual error involved in thinking about literary characters as if they were directly comparable to real people. Our most basic intuitions about how the world makes sense are simply not applicable to the figures that inhabit literary works, or at least the works of Shakespeare.

II Real people and make-believe people

In *Mimesis as Make-Believe* (1990), Kendall Walton proposes that works of art are most effectively understood by looking at children's games of make-believe and the 'props' typically used in such games. This represents a decisive shift away from the idea that a literary work is a text, or 'just words on a page'. Works of art are a special class of object used in the form of social interaction known as making believe. Walton analyses games involving mud-pies and snow forts, along with the spontaneous improvisation 'that makes a bush a bear'. He considers 'make-belief' to be a basic attitude that differs sharply from the various forms of untruth. A child playing with a doll doesn't just *think* the doll is a baby. In the framework of making believe, the doll is a baby. Many voyages of the starship *Enterprise* were successfully completed in the basement of our house on Grosvenor Avenue during the 1970s. The children engaged in playing these games are not confused about the difference between dolls and babies, nor do they intend to deceive others when they report they have gone where no one has gone before. 'This is my baby' and 'this is the starship *Enterprise*' are true statements in the fictional worlds they have created.

'The poet nothing affirmeth'. Walton's basic intuition about fiction is nicely anticipated in Sir Philip Sidney's *Apologie for Poetrie* (1595). Poetic utterances are not assertions and poets do not intend to solicit belief in what they say. Sidney is quite apologetic about poetry in his 'apologie', out of deference to Plato's notorious denunciation of poetry as a dangerous and seductive lie. Walton's 'defense of poetry' is a good deal more spirited. He is concerned with contemporary analytic philosophers who are made uncomfortable by the equivocal status of fictional utterances that are neither 'flesh, nor fowl, nor good red herring'. He is even more concerned to defend fiction from those theorists who insist that works of art are just black marks on a white surface, or oozings of paint on canvas. Fictional worlds have 'objective integrity worthy of the real world . . . making their exploration an adventure of discovery and surprise' (Walton 1990: 67).

The ability to negotiate successfully between beliefs and make-beliefs is for the most part acquired in early childhood, and indeed children are typically very skilful at these shifts. Sometimes, however, the subtle modulations required to make these transitions can go wrong. When our daughter was a baby we arranged day care for her with a neighbour. It was a barter arrangement that impoverished graduate students make, where we paid for day-care services by driving our neighbour to the supermarket. I came home one day to pick up the baby, who had not yet achieved the rank of starship captain, and was greeted at the door by the neighbours' four-year-old daughter Margaret. She presented me with a tray and said, 'Here Mister Bristol, we made cookies today'. Like a good, jolly parent I scooped up a cookie, popped it in my mouth, and exclaimed how delicious it was as I swallowed it. Margaret's eyes got very big: 'Oh Mister Bristol, those were make-believe cookies!' I guess the iridescent blue colour should have tipped me off. The 'cookies' were made out of Play-Doh and the taste was so vile I felt nauseated for the next twenty-four hours. The point of course is that I had somehow missed the cue that the cookies were props in a game of make-believe. But of course the situation could have been much worse. I might have said: 'Margaret, don't be silly. You're confusing Play-Doh characters with real cookies. When you become an English professor you'll realize that this is a mistake.' This response would have been socially maladroit and even downright mean. But it would also have been philosophically unjustified. 'We made cookies today' is a true statement in the fictional world of Play-Doh. The correct response when one is offered make-believe cookies, even blue ones, is to make believe eating them.

The attitude of make-believe is characterized both by correct understanding of certain complex stipulations and by the way those stipulations are taken up in relation to the background knowledge of everyday life. So in order correctly to enter into the game of make-believe cookies I must identify the stipulation that these lumps of Play-Doh are cookies. To participate fully in this game, I must contrive actions appropriate to cookie-eating. To do this I have to have reliable background knowledge of what a cookie is, how it comes into being, its typical fate and so on. In addition to all of this, moreover, I have to respect constraints on the make-believe, which in this case takes the form of the imperative: 'Don't eat the Play-Doh.' Make-believe is an activity where the basic stipulations – this is my baby, this is the starship *Enterprise*, these are cookies – are mandated arbitrarily by one or more 'authors'. But make-believe is never, strictly speaking, autonomous. Intelligent participation depends not only on shared agreement about the fictional terms of the game, but also and equally on the shared background knowledge of the participants.

Walton acknowledges that make-believe can be a heterogeneous mix of things that are contingently true in the real world and things that are contingently false. Duncan was king of Scotland and Macbeth did murder him in both the real world and in Shakespeare's play. But the real Duncan was a weak king and Macbeth apparently ruled Scotland wisely during his reign. According to the chronicles, Lady Macbeth was a widow and Macbeth was her second husband, but no such fact appears in Shakespeare's play. At the time *Macbeth* was written, many extraordinary beliefs about witches were commonly accepted as true. But we now know that most of these beliefs were malicious as well as false and that witches of the kind imagined in seventeenth-century texts have never existed. If, as Walton argues, the purpose of an artefact like *Macbeth* is to enable participation in a serious and sophisticated make-believe, how do the participants decide what they need to know in order to play the game as intelligently as possible? How do readers co-ordinate what they understand to be part of the make-believe proper (Macbeth visits the witches) with what they know to be true in the real world (witches don't exist)?

The classic analysis of this problem is an essay by David Lewis called simply 'Truth in fiction' (1983). Lewis predicates his discussion on the view that: 'Storytelling is pretence. The storyteller purports to be telling the truth about matters whereof he has knowledge' (1983: 266). However, since the author's pretence does not flow from an intention to deceive, fictions are not simply forms of untruth. Fictions are not true at our world, but they are true in possible worlds where they are told as known fact. Lewis begins with a proposal he calls Analysis 0: '*A sentence of the form "In fiction* f, φ*" is true iff* φ *is true at every world where* f *is told as known fact rather than fiction*' (1983: 268). Lewis goes on to gloss this in more informal terms:

> Is that right? There are some who never tire of telling us not to read anything into a fiction that is not there explicitly, and Analysis 0 will serve to capture the usage of those who hold this view in its most extreme form. I do not believe, however, that such a usage is at all common. Most of us are content to read a fiction against a background of well-known fact, 'reading into' the fiction content that is not there explicitly but that comes jointly from the explicit content and factual background.
>
> (p. 268)

Analysis 0 has much in common with the sort of position advocated by L. C. Knights. Lewis does not claim that the 'explicit content only' rule is wrong, only that it is not common. But it's hard to see how anyone could really understand a fiction by following the strict requirements of Analysis 0, since there are unstated presuppositions that are necessary for understanding any story. The problem is not to find a way to suppress all outside knowledge when reading a story, but rather how correctly to determine what, of all the things we might know, is really pertinent.

One way that people have of understanding stories is just to rely on their default knowledge of the world as it is. Lewis calls this Analysis 1; in formal terms it can be spelled out as follows:

> *A sentence of the form 'In the fiction* f, φ*' is non-vacuously true iff some world where* f *is told as known fact and* φ *is true differs less from our actual world, on balance, than does any world where* f *is told as known fact and* φ *is not true. It is vacuously true iff there are no possible worlds where* f *is told as known fact.*

(p. 270)

Informally this is equivalent to saying that what is true in a fiction depends on the co-ordination of explicit textual content with contingent matters of fact. To understand *Romeo and Juliet* you need to know what it's like when teenagers fall in love. This is the attitude adopted by people who say: 'My father-in-law is like King Lear' or 'Lady Macbeth must have had a child or else she wouldn't talk to her husband that way about suckling a baby'. Analysis 1 works well in many situations, but it is not without problems. For one thing, there are as many sets of 'contingent matters of fact' as there are possible readers of any story. And contingent matters of fact are constantly changing. As the chronological gap between a storyteller and a reader widens, basic facts that were important for understanding the story are lost, forgotten, or superseded by new kinds of knowledge. As an alternative to this proposal, then, Lewis offers something that more closely resembles a historicist solution.

One way to specify the background knowledge that can be most usefully deployed in relation to the explicit content of a literary work is to reconstruct the '*collective belief worlds of the community of origin*' (p. 273). This proposal results in Analysis 2:

> *A sentence of the form 'In the fiction* f, φ*' is non-vacuously true iff, whenever* w *is one of the collective belief worlds of the community of origin of* f*, then some world where* f *is told as known fact and* φ *is true differs less from the world* w*, on balance, than does any world where* f *is told as known fact and* φ *is not*

true. It is vacuously true iff there are no possible worlds where f *is told as known fact.*

(p. 273)

This proposal differs from Analysis 1 in demanding that readers somehow put aside their own background beliefs and at the same time amass specific knowledge of a historically distant context of beliefs and attitudes. What is true about London in the stories about Sherlock Holmes pretty much depends on what London was like at the time Conan Doyle was writing, not on what it is like for contemporary readers. On this account the theory of humours can be used to help explain Hamlet's behaviour, but psychoanalysis cannot. Analysis 2 would rule out vernacular statements like 'King Lear is just like my wife's father', on the grounds that social phenomena such as ageing and fatherhood are historically specific to the seventeenth-century context in which Shakespeare was writing. The 'naive' impression of a similarity between King Lear and my wife's father is false because it is based on ignorance of what fathers were really like in the historical setting in which Shakespeare's play was created. It is also an ideological manifestation, flowing from wishful thinking where readers prefer to believe that their own historically limited experience represents a transhistorical truth of some kind.

As a matter of principle many scholars strongly prefer some version of historicism (Analysis 2) to any uninstructed vernacular orientation (Analysis 1), even in cases where ideas like 'authorial intention' and 'original meaning' are no longer considered useful as a description of what scholarship is trying to find out. David Lewis, however, sees no compelling philosophical reason to favour either one of his two alternatives over the other. The historicist solution, Analysis 2, has some of the same problems as a vernacular approach, Analysis 1. Analysis 2 doesn't really provide any more reliable way to select what is relevant background knowledge for understanding a story than Analysis 1. There are as many beliefs circulating in the community of origin as there are contingent matters of fact in the actual world of contemporary readers. More immediately for the purposes of this chapter, there is nothing in Analysis 2 that can help with the problem of Lady Macbeth's children. There are many sets of beliefs specific to seventeenth-century society that help determine the background for reading *Macbeth*: beliefs about witches, beliefs about kings, beliefs about gender and sexuality. But none of these beliefs has any particular bearing on whether or not Lady Macbeth has had a child.

In *The Nature of Fiction* (1990), Gregory Currie argues that storytelling is not a derivative form of some other type of utterance. It is a basic discursive practice in its own right, different from but no less important than the truthful propositions of philosophers or historians. Like Walton, Currie in effect views fiction as a social practice or institution. Make-believe represents a specific intention on the part of an author to engage with readers in a co-operative form of social interaction or communicative game. 'The reader of fiction is invited by the author to engage in a game of make-believe, the structure of the game being in part dictated by the text of the author's work' (1990: 70). But the 'text of the author's work' can achieve its communicative purpose only if it is read with certain background assumptions. For Currie the reader's default assumptions are not the most reliable guide to appropriate participation in the game of make-believe devised by the author. Fiction is interactive, but author and reader do not participate on an equal footing nor do they have interchangeable roles. What is true in a particular fiction is what the author intends the reader to take for true, even when this entails the existence of witches, giant sandworms or wealthy vampires living quietly in suburban neighbourhoods. The most important tool for understanding any story, therefore, is the actual text provided for readers by the author. But the story communicated may depend more on what the author believes than on what may be a contingent matter of fact in the reader's world.

Currie does not recommend a stricter version of Lewis's Analysis 2 where the beliefs of an individual author are privileged over the more diffuse 'belief world of the community of origin'. Deciding what background knowledge is necessary for an intelligent response requires a grasp of what kind of story the author is telling. A familiarity with other stories is important as a background for understanding any fiction. This 'inter-fictional' background represents the specialized experience of readers as readers. Giant sandworms exist in *Dune* (1966) because Frank Herbert intends to tell a science fiction story, just as suburban vampires exist in *The Tale of the Body Thief* (1992) because Anne Rice wants to tell a horror story. Unfortunately, knowing what kind of story Shakespeare intended to tell in *Macbeth* doesn't help settle the question of Lady Macbeth's child any more effectively than the research programmes of historicism can. *Macbeth* is something like a horror story where as a contingent matter of fact witches actually exist, but *Macbeth* is also a historical chronicle. In both kinds of story, however, certain ontological principles, notably causality, remain in force. And there is no warrant in either genre for accepting a situation where it is both true and untrue that Lady Macbeth is a mother. Here the vernacular alternative has a decided advantage over more sophisticated levels of reading competence: Lady Macbeth talks about her child in the first act, but later in the play we learn that Macbeth has no children. The baby must have died; I wonder what happened to him.

Personally I find this more satisfying than the admittedly ingenious proposal worked out by Peter Stallybrass. Stallybrass provides a worthwhile account of the play's symbolic valances, but his argument requires acceptance of the logical contradiction of a child that both does and does not exist. But there is nothing in *Macbeth* that really forces anyone to pay this price. It is quite possible to interpret Lady Macbeth as a bad mother and a witch without introducing the metaphysical impossibility of an existing/non-existing child. But the reasoning that infers the death of Lady Macbeth's child by relating explicit textual prompts to ordinary, everyday background knowledge of the world does not represent a better theoretical solution to the problem, because it swaps a logical contradiction in the story with a logical fallacy in its interpretation.

> Strictly speaking, it is fallacious to reason from a mixture of truth in fact and truth in fiction . . . But in practice the fallacy is often not so bad. The factual premises in mixed reasoning may be part of the background against which we read fiction. They may carry over into the fiction, not because there is anything explicit in the fiction to make them true, but rather because there is nothing to make them false.
>
> (Lewis 1983: 269)

There is nothing in *Macbeth* to make it false that Lady Macbeth's child has died, certainly by the end of the play, and possibly even earlier, perhaps before the action of the story begins. Her lost child is as much part of the story of *Macbeth* as the lost Mammilius is part of the story of *The Winter's Tale*.

It makes better sense to make believe Lady Macbeth's child died of unknown causes rather than to make believe that the child she suckled never existed at all. The former view is no worse than the latter in its ability to bring out the internal complexity of Shakespeare's text; it may even be an improvement. Lady Macbeth is not only a bad mother, as Stallybrass argues, she is also a bereaved mother. The loss of a child is one of the elements that shapes and defines her character.

Macbeth: How does your patient, Doctor?
Doctor: Not so sick, my Lord,
        As she is troubled with thick-coming fancies,
        That keep her from her rest.
Macbeth: Cure her of that:
        Canst thou not minister to a mind diseas'd;
        Pluck from the memory a rooted sorrow;
        Raze out the written troubles of the brain;
        And with some sweet oblivious antidote

Cleanse the stuff'd bosom of that perilous stuff
Which weighs upon the heart?

(V. iii. 37–45)

The sorrow rooted in Lady Macbeth's brain is her remorse for the killing of Duncan. But sorrow can refer to ineradicable grief as well as to being sorry for something you have done. Instead of seeing Lady Macbeth as the symbolic manifestation of an ideological formation – in this case the 'anti-family' of witches – it is possible to 'read her character' as a mother who has suffered the loss of a child. On this view Lady Macbeth is not an abstract symbol of evil, or of the unnatural, but rather a person who commits an evil deed. Is it really more useful to consider this deed as the unmotivated malice of a witch rather than as the desperate act of an unhappy woman?

Lady Macbeth's child cannot be fully accounted for, no matter how carefully the text of *Macbeth* is studied. This leaves critics with a dilemma: accept an ontological contradiction in the story or a fallacy in its interpretation. There are no drop-dead arguments in favour of either way of doing things. It is effective to focus on the symbolic complexity of the text, even if this means the story is internally self-contradictory. But trying to piece out gaps in the story by reasoning from mixed premises can also be a productive way to participate in Shakespeare's make-believe. Historically speaking it has been far more common for people to focus greater attention on an effort to grasp the author's story in the fullest possible detail. Participation in the institution of make-believe is not a closed, self-referential pastime. Full engagement in make-believe is part of a larger commitment to ethical and political reflection.

3
On the need for a differentiated theory of (early) modern subjects
HUGH GRADY

I

In what follows I focus on the topic of subjectivity as it was conceptualized in Shakespeare studies in the 1980s under the influence of the theories of Michel Foucault and Louis Althusser. I believe these theories have led to impasses in our notions of early modern subjectivity.[1] I have discussed these weaknesses in general terms in earlier works, under a number of different headings (Grady 1991: 14–20, 225–45 and Grady 1996: 8–20, 213–19). In this context, however, I want to summarize and build on these earlier writings to define what I think has become something of a consensus, at least among a segment of critics, on the weaknesses of the approaches to subjectivity within those parts of feminism, new historicism and cultural materialism most influenced by French post-structuralist views on the subject. In the process, I will make the case for a different set of theoretical notions to help us 'think' subjectivity in terms that are open to its critical and creative potentialities as well as to its construction within a realm of ideology and power. For these purposes, I believe, writings of the Frankfurt School deserve more attention than they have hitherto enjoyed.[2]

Catherine Belsey's influential *Subject of Tragedy* (1985) is a representative instance of new historicist, cultural materialist and/or feminist theory developed from themes of Foucault and Althusser. Because the account that follows is mostly a negative one, let me be explicit here in stating my appreciation for Belsey's book as a finely chiselled and valuable product of a critical movement that has done much to further the cause of critical and political thinking in Shakespeare studies. Belsey's *The Subject of Tragedy*, like Francis Barker's related *The Tremulous Private Body* (1984), was a pioneering and scandalous work, a crucial instance of a broader movement within British academic criticism which challenged many long-held, dubious assumptions of academic literary criticism by using certain post-structuralist themes to put entrenched older critical practices under a new and much needed critical scrutiny.[3] My suggestions for a different approach to the problems this movement raises signal in fact my own sense of the importance of its contributions.

In *The Subject of Tragedy* Althusser is not directly cited (he is central in Belsey's earlier book, *Critical Practice* (1980)), but the framework of the book is clearly indebted to the Foucault of *The Order of Things* (Belsey 1985: 14), and theoretical borrowings from Foucault seem to merge seamlessly in this work with themes derived from the Althusserian Marxism of her earlier book, even though there are important differences between Foucault and Althusser, starting with Foucault's rejection of Marxism and Althusser's embracing of it. For example, Foucault's accounts of the early modern period had famously problematized modernization in ways even more critical than Marx and Engels' celebrated double-edged diagnosis in *The Communist Manifesto* and subsequent works. While Marx saw modernity as a process which would ultimately liberate humankind from oppression, it emerges for Foucault with much less positive coloration in the form of a 'disciplinary society' in which a technology of surveillance, epitomized by the figure of the Panopticon, regulates society in its inequality and authoritarianism through prisons, schools, hospitals, the military and the factory, culminating in mass internalization of the identities or selves created by these institutions (Foucault 1979). Employing the Nietzschean notion that behind every ideal can be discovered strategies of domination, Foucault sardonically identified this objectified construct of the technology of power with the humanist subject. The polemical intent of this terminology was clear: it was part of a generational assault on a French philosophical tradition focused on the problem of the subject – and in that sense imbued with 'humanism' – since Montaigne and Descartes, and palpably so during the high tide of Sartre and the humanist Marxism which dominated much of French intellectual life from the 1940s through to the 1960s. It was an assault conducted in the name of a new structuralist concept of knowledge emphasizing limits, materiality, science and other related antitheses to the ideologies of freedom, transcendence and hermeneutics associated with the previous age of existentialism.[4] It was also encouraged by Martin Heidegger's protest (since amplified by Derrida) against Sartre's interpretation of Heidegger as belonging within this older 'humanist' tradition. Heidegger rejected the label 'humanist' for his own reasons, but his arguments encouraged similar protests by structuralists who otherwise had little in common with Heidegger's mystical philosophy of Being (Rockmore 1995: 40–80 *passim*).

Quoting Foucault's *The Order of Things* on the historicity of the concept of 'man', Belsey imports the term 'liberal humanism' into the opening paragraphs of Part 1 of her study as its central concept. She offers no other commentary on its provenance. This relative silence has created unintended but real problems. In the case of words as protean and indeterminate in meaning as both 'humanism' and 'liberal', any reader, and especially one removed in time or space from Belsey's point of composition, is left with a number of theoretical questions about her central term. Readers can never be completely certain as to the theoretical domain from which the argument is drawing its categories and narratives – although clearly materials from (unidentified) Marxist, post-structuralist and feminist discourses are grafted on to the (apparently) Foucauldian framework.

To take one problem, just what kind of mental entity *is* liberal humanism? At points it acts exactly like Marxian ideology: like ideology, it 'was produced in the interests of the bourgeois class . . . in the second half of the seventeenth century' (Belsey 1985: 7), and it is productive of misleading, inequality-justifying ideas; thus liberal humanism appears at this point to be a set of ideas of the sort that Marx in *The German Ideology* (1947) defined and critiqued. But whereas Marx situated 'ideology' within theoretical attempts to rationalize and justify the status quo by proto-professional writers (in line with Napoleon's early use of the term to dismiss impractical theorists), Belsey's 'liberal humanism' shows signs at other points of having become that transformed version of ideology theorized by Althusser, much more like 'culture' in the anthropological sense, 'pre-structuring' experience for the subject – and in fact constituting the subject itself – in ways of which the subject was unaware.[5] Like Althusserian ideology, liberal humanism constructs an idea of the self which becomes interiorized by its subjects (Belsey 1985: 5–6). But Althusser's very briefly sketched theory (Althusser 1971; see also Althusser 1977: 233–4) was only one of several similar theories of the subject spawned by French structuralism/post-structuralism. The best-known of these, besides Althusser's, were Foucault's and Lacan's, both of which also made attempts to politicize the structuralist idea that language is a self-enclosed, reality-constituting system. These three theorists, however, used different and disparate terms to 'name' the socializing mental medium in question: ideology for Althusser; episteme, discourse and power/ knowledge for Foucault; and symbolic order for Lacan. Belsey's 'liberal humanism' has affinities with all of these – which fact may explain why 'liberal humanism' is always referred to as such in the text of *The Subject of Tragedy*, never categorized as either ideology, discourse, episteme or any of the other possible terms. Like these three variants of French structuralism/ post-structuralism, Belsey's liberal humanism constructs a sense of selfhood or subjectivity which is experienced as a self by its subjects, but which is illusory in the sense that (Belsey asserts) subjectivity is an effect of language (and presumably its specialized construct, liberal humanism), not self-creating and autonomous as it seems to be to its subjects (Belsey 1985: 5–6).

But this idea of a socially constructed self formed in a (somewhat indeterminate) socio-mental medium – language/ideology/episteme – leaves us with a fundamental theoretical problem, raised by many critics in connection with Althusser and Foucault: how can we account for cases in which the self manages to step outside of the determining mentality in order to criticize and change it? There is one possible answer in *The Subject of Tragedy*: Belsey refers to Derridean ideas of textuality as offering gaps within language which open it up to contestation and resistance: 'Since meaning is plural, to be able to speak is to be able to take part in the contest for meaning which issues in the production of new subject-positions, new determinations of what it is possible to be' (1985: 6). But these openings, though real enough, seem to me very narrow cracks from which to prise the fundamental revolutions and conflicts with which human history is replete. To my mind the mentalities of modernity must be seen as more fundamentally fragmentary if we are to account for the innumerable conflicts which have characterized previous and present history. And if we were to bring into the picture the seminal work of psychoanalyst Jacques Lacan, an important 'source' for Althusser and an indirect one for Foucault, we would end by significantly calling into question Belsey's supposition of a self constructed entirely in language.[6] For Lacan language is, indeed, of great importance. But so too is the pre-linguistic, specular Imaginary order which constitutes, as it were, its own 'self' (the *moi* or 'ego' in Lacan's terms) separate from the self of language, the *je* (Lacan 1979). And without the *moi*, the *je* or speaking self, according to one of Lacan's premier interpreters to the Anglophone world, 'would otherwise be a neutral automaton, mouthing the clichés and conventions of a given culture' (Ragland-Sullivan 1987: 59). This automaton-like status – to come directly to the point of this critique – is the lugubrious condition which Belsey's Althusserian/Foucauldian idea of a self constituted solely by and in language/ideology/discourse tends to. It is an idea, we will see, which Belsey resolutely resists in the second half of the book after putting it in place in the first half.

In short, Belsey's 'liberal humanism' is an ideology, episteme and/or power/knowledge nexus constructed from Foucauldian and Althusserian materials, and it is implicated in all the problems of its two disparate progenitors, who each have attempted to reduce human subjectivity to an effect of power in ways which lock us into inescapable iron cages of social stasis.

As Jürgen Habermas once put it in an understated critique of this tradition, it is as if humans were unable to learn from their experiences with mental frameworks and undertake modifications of them (Habermas 1987b: 320–1).

Whatever its other ambiguities, 'liberal humanism' clearly acts as the kind of static framework Habermas criticized. It is defined as 'the ruling assumptions, values and meanings of the modern epoch' (Belsey 1985: 7), and it is said to constitute 'the consensual orthodoxy of the west' (Belsey 1985: ix), proposing among other things that 'the subject is the free unconstrained author of meaning and action, the origin of history' (Belsey 1985: 8). But this heavily weighted, central concept of 'liberal humanism' finally collapses, I will argue, because it tries to unify too many contradict-ory, differentiated social practices within an imprisoning functionalism. In short, it ignores to the point of undermining its own logical cogency the kinds of fissures and dissociations of rationality through which, in Frankfurt and post-Frankfurt theory, were constructed all the different versions of fissured modern subjects and modern, differentiated rationality – some of which turn out to be crucial resources of resistance against the impersonal power structures of modernity. Modernity has involved such crucial divi-sions as the split between instrumental rationality and irrational emotion; between the different modes of knowledge which make up modern aca-demic disciplines and, fundamentally, between public and private selves. However, instead of defining these divisions of knowledge and of the self central to modernity, Belsey ends up in a chimerical quest for a single inclusive ideology/episteme to account for the post-medieval West. Thus, I believe, her argument imposes on 'liberal humanism' the same kind of impossible unity which she believes a unitary liberal humanism imposes on its conception of the subject. In short, the concept of 'liberal humanism' calls for the same kind of questioning of its supposed unity as Belsey's own critique undertook in relation to *its* subject. The unity assumed in the vari-ous Western myths of 'humanist' subjectivity is in this theory displaced onto what I believe is an equally mythical unitary liberal humanism.

I should stress that the unity of Belsey's category 'liberal humanism' is not so much argued as implied by the repetition of the same term to cover a number of disparate functions. For example, liberal humanism was appar-ently constructed piece by piece, in disparate epistemic contexts: it doesn't come into systematic existence, we learn from a number of different pas-sages, until the second half of the seventeenth century. On the other hand, there was a clearly defined medieval self, extracted almost entirely by Belsey from the late medieval morality plays, and this medieval self is replaced by something significantly different in the age of Shakespeare, well before the emergence of systematic liberal humanism. What this something different turns out to be, interestingly enough, is a conflictual temporal period (more or less co-extensive with what orthodox literary history calls the English Renaissance) in which there is a contest among a residual medieval self, an absolutist ideology and a yet-to-be-fully-formed liberal humanist self. The result appears in complex texts like the plays of Marlowe and Shakespeare.

Beyond these complications, there are at least three distinct types of subjectivity uneasily grouped by Belsey under the 'liberal humanist' umbrella. In Belsey's historical narrative, these were formed at discrete historical junctures, so that they are in that sense already differentiated (as I believe they should be). Nevertheless they are all labelled as aspects of a unitary liberal humanism which happen to arise at different historical moments. The first, clearly a part of the Renaissance, is that associated with Hamlet, Milton's Satan, the Duchess of Malfi and a number of others, and it is a liberal humanism defined by (an apparently new) 'interiority' seen as 'author and origin of meaning and choice' (Belsey 1985: 35). The second is also present in the Renaissance, but primarily in the objectifying methods of Francis Bacon. And Bacon is seen as a precursor of a more historically consequential and much later exponent of objectification, the late seventeenth-century empirical philosopher John Locke. This second mode of liberal humanism creates science and positive concepts generally through an instrumental language (Belsey 1985: 83), which acts as the spearhead of an equally instrumental reason.

Finally, there is a third mode of humanism, also exemplified by Locke, but, I would argue, one that is logically different from either of the other two. In his celebrated *Second Treatise of Government* and *Essay Concerning Human Understanding* (both 1689), Locke posits an autonomous, natural self, endowed with certain inalienable rights. Of course, Locke made the right to own property pre-eminent among these rights and thus became one of the great ideologues of a rapidly maturing capitalism. This conception of the self seems to me quite distinct from those of selves of interiority like Hamlet, whose problem was precisely how to find a place within an alien world; nor again is this the same as the subject-position of instrumental reason, which occludes all values other than those of domination and control. Locke's political self on the contrary is a juridical fiction which retrospectively appears to have been a necessary and theoretical construct of a new bourgeois social order in post-Restoration England. It was one with few if any precursors in Shakespeare's England, precisely because it emerged as a new ideological groundwork for bourgeois-democratic society, and it proved to be *the* historical answer to the crisis of legitimacy which, *pace* Jonathan Dollimore and numerous others, slowly unfolded in the sixteenth and seventeenth centuries. This new discourse utilized older natural law philosophy with a new and radical critique of absolutism to ground society in a 'social contract' rather than through God's deputized authority. There had certainly been earlier incipient critiques of absolutism, as many have argued over several decades. But the crucial elements of Locke's discourse that allow it to function as the kind of central ideology of the sort Belsey posits seem to me to lie far in the future, Bacon's instrumental writings notwithstanding.

Rather than go further into the specific problems raised by Althusser's and Foucault's theories of subjectivity,[7] I believe it will be more useful to try to outline what a post-post-Althusserian, 'supplemented' Foucauldian theory of subjectivity would have to accomplish in order to gain general acceptance.[8]

1 The strength of Foucault's and Althusser's approaches lies in their appreciation that post-Enlightenment Western culture created a number of central myths about itself. Among these was a set of notions concerning individuality and subjectivity which has often worked to valorize a category of the individual that supposedly transcended or made morally irrelevant disparities of wealth and power.

2 While recognizing that the self is created within languages, institutions and families that are in turn permeated with all the socially created disparities alluded to above, it is necessary as well to grant an area of relatively autonomous psychological structuring seen to include unconscious, non-rational processes. Frederick Crewes notwithstanding,[9] I don't see any alternative to the various versions of Freudian psychoanalysis which are a strong component of contemporary Shakespeare (and other cultural) studies – and which of course inherently stress the family as a socializing institution.

3 The great weakness of both Foucault and Althusser is their tendency to make subjectivity a purely passive outcome of determinate social forces, thereby paradoxically replicating positivist social science. Here, I think, the Marxist tradition's own overdetermined blindspots – its reductionist, systematizing tendencies – contribute to the problem, reinforcing Foucault's and Althusser's failures adequately to theorize the possibilities of critical rationality, of subaltern communities of resistance, and of utopian thinking and action. Thus it will be necessary for renewed materialist theories of subjectivity to create an account of agency, of the potentially creative, power-resisting activity of the self within the world – without at the same time regressing to myths of complete individual autonomy from the social.

4 A renewed theory of subjectivity should be resolutely historical, suspicious of what I take to be another area of weakness in Belsey's *The Subject of Tragedy*, which in effect collapses three centuries of cultural

history within a single, three-centuries-old episteme or ideology of liberal humanism.[10] On the contrary, every self is an outcome of complex psycho-historical processes, and while the selves of specific cultures and societies share socially constructed discourses and ideologies, they are by no means identical or interchangeable, differing significantly through both historical change and individual variations within historical epochs. Our accounts of the history of the self should accordingly be nuanced and open to the complexity of historical and individual differences.

II

The history of the self is involved in a set of consequential contingencies of quite lengthy historical provenance, and it can't be reduced to the effect of a single ideology or discursive formation. Important qualities defined by Belsey as components of the 'liberal humanist self', Charles Taylor has argued, were actually constituted in the late Roman empire, in the complex changes effected by Christianization (Taylor 1989), changes which are partially traceable in the text of Augustine's *Confessions*.[11] This is a topic, in fact, which I believe was opened up in Stephen Greenblatt's *Renaissance Self-fashioning* that has somehow got lost in the complexity of reactions to and developments of this paradigm-reconfiguring book. Greenblatt began, he says in his Introduction (1980: 1–9), by telling stories of a transformed self, but he discovered that the transformations, far from being autonomous and self-determining, as in the mythical, concept-creating nineteenth-century documents of Burckhardt and Michelet, in fact were implicated in the simultaneous transformation of Western culture into a system for colonizing much of the globe. But this second discovery proved so powerful, even explosive, in its implications for writing about Renaissance literature in general that further exploration of Greenblatt's first topic, the fashioning of the self, in a certain sense got indefinitely postponed, and his apparent affiliations with the pessimistic accounts of power and ideology from the 'structuralist' Foucault and Althusser took precedence in the reception of his book over his theories of the aesthetic and the subjective. In fact I think Greenblatt has a subtler and more nuanced sense of the problematics of selfhood than we find in Belsey or Barker, one derived from his early immersion in versions of Western Marxism which he has described on several occasions, but which are largely missing from the narrower theoretical world of the strand of British post-structuralism being developed by Belsey and Barker.[12]

I believe that a number of the widely desired qualities of an adequate theory of subjectivity in fact already exist where Greenblatt began, in the form of the unorthodox Marxist writings of Raymond Williams, Antonio Gramsci and, perhaps most outstandingly, in the so-called Critical Theory[13] of Max Horkheimer, Theodor Adorno, Walter Benjamin and Jürgen Habermas – sources, however, which were downplayed in the reception of Greenblatt and otherwise neglected during the post-structuralist heyday of the late 1970s and early 1980s. Of course themes from these sources in turn would have to be opened up to insights from feminism and French post-structuralism. But it is precisely in the area of subjectivity that the strengths of Frankfurt School Critical Theory (and of Williams and Gramsci as well) are most apposite, the weaknesses of post-structuralism most apparent.

Unfortunately, it is not as if a Frankfurt School theory of the subject and a clairvoyant critique of post-structuralist subjectivity exist ready-made. Charles Taylor's massive *Sources of the Self* (1989) makes extensive use of Frankfurt themes, but he combines them with more 'orthodox' philo-sophical and historical analysis and cites the important Frankfurt source Max Weber as inspiring several crucial concepts of his own work, without much attention to the Frankfurt School's subsequent development of them. More explicitly indebted to Frankfurt theory are Peter Dews (1987) and Anthony Giddens (1991), each of whom has done some admirable work in inserting Frankfurt themes into current post-structuralist debates. In add-ition, Fredric Jameson has laboured over his entire career to inject such thinking into his wide-ranging theoretical constructs,[14] while Terry Eagleton has done so outstandingly in more recent years.[15] But this work is compli-cated by the age of the classic texts involved, which are redolent of mid-century Modernism and post-Nazi political despair. In addition, there is the initially opaque, forbidding quality of much Frankfurt writing, including the classic work most relevant here, Horkheimer and Adorno's jointly written *Dialectic of Enlightenment* (1972), but also most of Adorno's other, seminal writing. This forbidding quality is a result, first, of a self-conscious belief that 'easy' writing has by its nature already succumbed to ideology and reification, and, second, of the method of 'negative dialectics' itself, a refusal of any final syntheses or ultimate concrete totality, so that Adorno resists simple summary and single-minded clarity.[16] However, these are also the very qualities that make this body of work so valuable and relevant now in our post-deconstructive age, giving us a theory that is necessarily open-ended and unfinished but which can give us themes, insights, 'constellations' in Benjamin's suggestive phrase, rather than stable systems or 'scientific' concepts.

The most important point about this body of work for my purposes is that an appreciation for the creative potential of subjectivity has always coexisted with a recognition of subjectivity's powerful ties to the social. *Dialectic of Enlightenment* is one way into this theme. This work, written in

German in the USA in the 1940s, is a critique of the project of Enlightenment rationality, describing a 'myth of Enlightenment' widely accepted by
the leading forces of Western society since the eighteenth century, a myth
celebrating Western progress and rationality. However, as Horkheimer and
Adorno argued at the dawn of the atomic age, the Enlightenment produced
instead an earth which 'radiates disaster triumphant' (1972: 3). Enlightenment rationality produced an autonomous, value-free, instrumental rationality, entwined in a manner defying conventional notions of cause and effect
with a homologous, reified capitalist economy. The resulting 'purposeless
purposiveness' of instrumental reason and the dynamics of capitalism then
promoted a systematic organization of the world into forms of domination
by impersonal, autonomous power,[17] in a process called 'reification'. At the
same time, the Enlightenment objectification of nature and its critique of
religion allowed the production of forms of critical rationality and of
autonomous modern aesthetics, which became a kind of enclave against
instrumental rationality. *Dialectic of Enlightenment* approaches despair over
the possibilities for human emancipation that had previously been so central
to Marxist discourse. The working class, for example, appears principally as
a mere object of the manipulations of the new electronic culture industry.
But the book implicitly affirms the emancipative value of the very critical
rationality which constitutes its own defiant refusal of the emerging post-
Nazi world, so that while it is pessimistic, it does posit areas of resistance to
reification.

   This is a very short and partial summary of a rich book, but I want here
to focus on the issue of subjectivity. Because in this theory rationality is
'differentiated' into epistemologically distinct modes (instrumental, aesthetic
and critical[18]) and because 'aesthetics' is seen as contradictory, containing
both incentives to social reform and revolution as well as to quiescence and
abstention, and finally because the internalization of authority is seen not as
unitary (as it becomes for Foucault and Althusser), but as a complex process
mediated by the diverse structures and practices of families, creative of
different personality-types (Horkheimer 1972), subjectivity is explicitly contradictory and indeterminate, and it does not automatically justify the status
quo. It is not automatically 'ideological' although, as I indicated, Frankfurt
theorists famously grew more and more pessimistic about political change
as time went on. In fact, one of the most recurrent and lugubrious themes
elaborated by Adorno as he contemplated emerging mass media society in
America and then in Germany from the 1940s to the 1960s took the form
of a lament for the apparent disappearance of classic bourgeois individual
subjectivity, which culminated for him in the Victorian Age, and which for
all its much discussed failings had at least retained a certain capacity for
aesthetic judgement and rationality. But in the post-World War II era, it

now seemed to be succumbing to modern advertising and the mass media more generally, with their 'psycho-analysis in reverse' aimed at a general replacement of ego by id. And while most of us would back away from what seems now to be a too despairing appraisal of the annihilating power of the media over critical rationality, I doubt that many of us would completely dissent from Adorno's powerful account of its colonizing, de-politicizing capacities.

As this account suggests, the Frankfurt School, very early in its development, saw the need to supplement its Marxism with Freudian psycho-analysis (Jay 1984b: 203–5), and this fruitfully tension-filled, incomplete synthesis remains basic to its theorizing. As I mentioned earlier, however, it is often in accounts of the aesthetic that the potential resistances of post-Enlightenment subjects are most fully described in Frankfurt theory. In fact, as is well known, Adorno in particular began to believe that, in the face of what seemed to him clear co-optation of the working class within advanced capitalism, only modern artworks, with all their hermetic difficulties and complex textures, had escaped the colonizing effects of the otherwise all-pervasive processes of instrumentalization, reification and commodification of human life in advanced capitalism: the artworks, and, of course, the subjectivities which (in a complex process, partially conscious, partially unconscious, and mediating a social context) created and experienced them. But Adorno never understood jazz, nor the role of the African-American aesthetic in strands of American and now world popular culture, and I (and numerous others) believe that the most pessimistic and most 'Modernist' conclusions which he drew deserve to be revised in the light of additional decades of a new, postmodernist relation between high art and popular culture (cf. Eagleton 1990: 341–65).

Adorno's former student Jürgen Habermas can take us part of the way in this needed revision of Adorno. His reconceptualization of the process of commodification whose reifying effects Adorno had defined is an important theoretical development which helps create a conceptual space for understanding how oppressed people are able to resist the structures of domination which define their place in society. The key is his distinction between the 'lifeworld' (the historically formed communities in which everyday life is lived, language is spoken, meaning is created and subjectivity formed, and resistance can be both thought and enacted) and the realm of 'systems' (the non-linguistic, socially created, but reified, out-of-control networks constituted by the economy, state bureaucracies, the law, and institutionalized instrumental or technical rationality embodied in professions, corporations, the military, education and so on) (Habermas 1987a). This distinction allows us to theorize the continuing existence of meaning, value and practical rationality even in the worst-case scenario Adorno described: our own era of a highly advanced colonization of the lifeworld by reified systems. In fact in the very intersubjective constitution of the lifeworld resides an inherent resistance to the value-free, levelling and corrosive processes of reification, just as for Adorno the very sensuous and archaic nature of the artwork had allowed it to resist the commodifying effects of advanced capitalism. Thus the concept of the lifeworld can give us one of the most desired features of a revised materialist theory of the subject, a locus where the observed resistances to power and the forces of subjection can be theoretically grounded. In effect, Habermas has created the missing theory underlying E. P. Thompson's classic *The Making of the English Working Class* (1966), with its rich and specified understanding of a culture of resistance.

Unfortunately, Habermas has often suffered from an aesthetic 'tone deafness', whether we are speaking of his sometimes stodgy prose style, so different from that of Adorno's aesthetically self-conscious, dense and stylistically coruscating essays, or the relative banality of his few brief incursions into aesthetic topics. Thus Habermas doesn't so much supersede Adorno as provide a corrective for his political pessimism without either replacing or invalidating his aesthetic theory.[19] As Eagleton put it briefly in his very cogent and appreciatory discussion of Adorno in *The Ideology of the Aesthetic*, Adorno's political pessimism is probably responsible both for the richness of his elaboration of a fictional aesthetic realm and the paucity of his political theory (1990: 359). For Habermas the cases are precisely reversed.

Thus, if I may return to the list given earlier of the features necessary for a theory of subjectivity, I believe that in this rich and nuanced body of work are themes and ingredients that fulfil much of the case. This theory is foundationally social and political, it incorporates psychoanalytic theory and it recognizes the creative potential of subjectivity, as well as its embeddedness in the social. It is, I believe, in the area of historicizing and periodizing Frankfurt concepts of subjectivity that most work needs to be done. For Habermas and the Frankfurt School, the eighteenth-century Enlightenment, with its intertwined projects of capitalist economic 'take-off' and fissuring of rationality (to create the classical bourgeois self, the autonomy of art and the hegemony of a corrosive, value-free instrumental rationality), has been a historical turning point. In essence, the creation of two domains of purposeless purposiveness (the capitalist economy and autonomous, instrumental rationality), each implicated in a dynamic of ceaseless and unmotivated expansion and development, creates the crisis of modernity which, in the apocalyptic mid-twentieth-century climaxes of Nazism, Leninism, one-dimensional commodity culture and nuclear weapons, threatened the existence of humanity and human freedom – and continues to do so, less dramatically, in the changed circumstances of the post-Cold War era.

However, even though Horkheimer and Adorno in *Dialectic of Enlighten-ment* (and Foucault in his related theories of disciplinarity) focused on the Enlightenment as a crucial historical conjuncture for the creation of mod-ernity, their work also implies the existence of a number of other 'dialectics of enlightenment' at earlier moments of history. And of course the dynamic continues up to the present, with no sign of any abatement (cf. Jameson 1990: 100–10). My own recent work with four central Shakespearean plays (*Troilus and Cressida, Othello, King Lear* and *As You Like It*) has convinced me that Shakespeare's London theatre was itself a highly prescient abstract and chronicle of an emerging modernity in this sense (Grady 1996). Within Shakespeare's lifetime, London emerged as a centre for an embryonic commodity capitalism whose corrosive effects were already being com-mented on and represented theatrically (Bruster 1992), and recognition of this new social reality (along with a kind of despairing critique of it) is a central motif of *Troilus and Cressida, Timon of Athens* and (intertwined infer-nally with a cultural anti-Semitism) *The Merchant of Venice*. But Shakespeare's plays are more centrally concerned with two other modes of modernity-creating reification, autonomous from but interacting with the emerging capitalist economy. The first of these is instrumental rationality, treated as a double-edged sword of liberating 'distantiation' from the prevailing ideolo-gies of the day, but also as a destroyer of *all* values and human communities, as Horkheimer and Adorno argued in *Dialectic of Enlightenment*, and as we can see clearly in the cases of Iago, Edmund of *King Lear* and a number of other nihilistic malcontents.[20]

Partially overlapping with the theme of demythologized, instrumental rationality is another so large we have to step back to see it, and that is the area of 'Machiavellian' political dynamics so central to the tragedies and histories[21] – and not unknown in the comedies, with *As You Like It* and *The Tempest* clear examples of muted treatments of this theme. But to see the reified nature of power it is necessary to supplement an older rhetoric of 'moral evil' and to execute a shift of focus concerning the tragic heroes and heroines of these plays to reveal the ways in which heroism (now coded 'archaic' in this context) emerges against the foil of impersonal power politics embodied in icy characters – Claudius, Iago, Goneril and Regan, Cornwall, Octavius Caesar, for example – whose interiority amounts to little more than status as subject-positions for the playing out of the logics of reified power, reason and sexuality.

In a dynamic with which Shakespeare repeatedly experimented, the logic of reified power is paired dialectically with overdetermined, libidinized subjectivities in characters ranging from Richard II, Falstaff, Troilus and Cressida, Rosalind, Hamlet, Othello, Antony and Cleopatra, and Edgar, Cordelia and the transformed Lear.[22] Speaking very broadly, I would define the dynamics of this interaction as follows: through a kind of complicity between protagonists and antagonists, the cultural space of the play, as in both *Richard II* and *King Lear*, is evacuated of traditional worldviews or ideologies by a severing of the symbols of political legitimation from the actual exercise of power,[23] an operation which in one stroke empties the political ideology of its meaning and creates a new realm of nameless, reified power which proceeds to devastate the lifeworld of the play.

Versions of recognizably 'modern' subjectivity emerge in a number of forms in this dynamic, on the side of the disempowered and (initially deluded) characters, and such subjectivity is coded as unfettered, aimless, disconnected and alienated – but also suffused with libido and creative of some of the most remarkable insights, poetry and dramatic moments of these great plays.

In the dynamic between reified power and subjectivity in these plays, there is no question of ethical neutrality in the sense of morally equating, say, Hamlet and Claudius, Othello and Iago, Edgar and Edmund. If we have to choose, the drama leaves us no practical choice, given our own cultural continuities with the ethical world in which these texts were created, Terence Hawkes's demonstration of a subtext of a heroic Claudius within *Hamlet* notwithstanding (1985: 310–32). At the same time, however, I argue that we need to avoid a Romantic-Modernist coding that idealizes subjectivity as an absolute value of such transcendent eminence that a kind of 'moral' victory of good in the face of a worldly triumph of evil occurs. This all but dissolves the tragic force of the endings of *Hamlet*, *Othello* and *King Lear*, for example, and occludes the subtle critique of disembodied, 'modern' subjectivity which is also, I argue, a feature of these plays. In all of them – and more pointedly in the treatment of the subjective Trojans of *Troilus and Cressida* – modern subjectivity is disclosed as ungrounded and open to an arbitrary play of desire which becomes as corrosive and self-perpetuating as the reified power and instrumental rationality epitomized by *Troilus*'s Greeks and the other tragic villains. In *King Lear* and elsewhere, however, we learn that such subjectivity, in the guise of Cordelia, Edgar and the transformed Lear from the heath scenes on, is also the *locus* for the workings of the utopian – that recognition of the possibilities of redemption and amelioration evoked so often by Adorno and Benjamin and their more recent followers as an essential component of human being in the world.

In short, it appears to me that in this list of major Shakespearean works (and elsewhere in the period), we can discern in the Renaissance the dynamics of a dialectic of enlightenment before the Enlightenment proper. The double-edged analysis of this process, which simultaneously affirms the power and the disastrous potential of instrumental rationality, capitalist economics and the resulting play of autonomous power, also sees a portentous set of opportunities for both creativity and empty futility in the autonomous realms of subjectivity and the aesthetic set free in the complex process creative of a modernity which we still inhabit.

Notes

1 An earlier version of this chapter was prepared as a contribution to the seminar on 'Reconsidering subjectivity', co-chaired by Akiko Kusunoki and Valerie Wayne at the World Shakespeare Conference, Los Angeles, 9 April 1996.

2 For standard introductions to Frankfurt Critical Theory, see Jay 1973 and Held 1980; and for central Frankfurt theorists, see Jameson 1971. A very helpful, more recent study, focused around the concept of modernity, is Kellner 1989. The most comprehensive treatment, only recently available in English, is Wiggershaus 1994. Other important secondary sources will be cited below as the discussion develops.

3 See Easthope 1988 for a very useful study of this important critical strand; it includes a chapter on Belsey.

4 See Macey 1995: 170–82 for a recent and informative account of this dynamic and many details on the specific context for Foucault's use of the term 'humanism'.

5 See Belsey 1980: 56–84 for an earlier explication of the importance of Althusser's concept of ideology to her understanding of the subject and subjectivity. In an articulation which Belsey explicitly relates to the theory of *Screen* magazine (69), Althusser is related to interpretations of Lacan and Benveniste, but not in this text to Foucault.

6 In her earlier *Critical Practice* (1980) Belsey, like any number of the proponents of the post-Althusserian strand of British post-structuralism described by Easthope 1988, argued that Althusser's ideology worked like Lacan's linguistic 'symbolic order' (1980: 60–2, 64–6), concluding in a summarizing passage that: 'The subject is constructed in language and in discourse and, since the symbolic order in its discursive use is closely related to ideology, in ideology. It is in this sense that ideology has the effect, as Althusser argues, of constituting individuals as subjects . . .' (1980: 61). To my mind the move from language or the symbolic order to ideology is problematic (is language the same as ideology?), and the non-linguistic aspects of the decentred Lacanian self are not taken into account until later in the discussion (Belsey 1980: 64–5), when the unconscious is first mentioned in conjunction with a discussion of possible sources of distantiation from ideology. But this is the point at which I believe Lacan surpasses and undoes the monolithic hold of ideology over the subject in Althusser, in effect breaking with, rather than extending, Althusser. For a cogent and detailed argument sceptical of Althusser's attempted appropriation of aspects of Lacan, see Macey 1994.

7 For excellent discussions of these problems, see Dews 1995 and Elliott 1994. I give a more detailed critique of Althusser in Grady 1998.

8 Objections related to the ones I have discussed are raised and addressed, for example, in Charnes 1993, which, while it borrows Althusser's concept of interpellation, amends it radically by highlighting resistances to interpellation, at least in the special case of Shakespeare's legendary characters, Richard III, Troilus and Cressida, and Antony and Cleopatra. Similarly, recent works by

feminist Judith Butler (1990, 1993, 1997) focus on those aspects of French post-structuralism, especially within French feminism, which complicate or resist the idea of the subject as (only) a speaking being participating in the Lacanian symbolic order. See particularly Butler 1997: 24–41 for an audacious attempt to synthesize Althusser on interpellation with Austin on the speech-act.

9 Crewes has achieved some notoriety in the USA for a series of articles in *The New York Review of Books* in which he urged the speedy disposal of Freud and Freudianism into the proverbial dustbin of history.

10 Belsey recognized this problem, warning us of the dangers of 'collapsing the historical specificities and the ideological differences of three centuries into a single term' (1985: 7). However, I would argue, she in fact goes on to do so, and therein lie many of the book's problems.

11 See Taylor 1989: 127–42 for an extended treatment of Augustine's contributions to modern concepts of the self. In general Taylor approaches Belsey's topic of the construction of the modern self in much greater detail and over a much broader historical range through a depiction of a highly differentiated, multilayered, complex historical process.

12 This view of Greenblatt is expanded in Grady 1993.

13 The term highlights the importance of Kantian and Marxian critique to the method, which is centred in social theory and philosophy rather than literary criticism; however, aesthetics is a central topic in this tradition, and Adorno and Benjamin of course wrote many examples of what we would call (lower-case) critical theory and practice.

14 See especially Jameson 1990 and his earlier classic works, Jameson 1971 and Jameson 1981.

15 See especially Eagleton 1990.

16 See especially Adorno 1990. In addition to the works by Jameson cited above, see for introductions to this central concept of Adorno: Buck-Morss 1977; Rose 1978; Jay 1984a; and Jay 1984b; as well as Jay 1973, cited earlier.

17 The similarities with Foucault's later analysis of power in the post-Enlightenment West are clear; Foucault himself recognized them retrospectively; see Raulet 1983.

18 These categories were defined in a relatively early work, Habermas 1979, and Habermas has since modified them (and become more critical of what he sees as an untenable Nietzschean problematic in *Dialectic of Enlightenment*) in his 'linguistic turn'. But I find them useful ways of summarizing less systematically enunciated concepts of non-instrumental rationality in Horkheimer and Adorno.

19 Habermas, especially in Habermas 1987b: 106–30 *passim*, has put more distance between himself and Adorno than I am supposing here, tending to link Horkheimer and Adorno with French post-structuralists in not grasping the potential of communicative action as a counter-force to reification.

20 My argument here 'supplements' the treatment of Jacobean malcontents in Dollimore 1984 by arguing that Iago is the prototype of a much more negative malcontent than the ones Dollimore treats. These malcontents, as Dollimore asserts, do indeed reveal the prevailing ideologies of Elizabethan and Jacobean England as ideology, but they go on to reveal that the cleared space of disenchanted rationality which they create is itself the arena for new kinds of reifications, most notably an instrumental rationality which becomes

self-perpetuating and corrosive of both 'old' and 'new' values. For further details of this argument, see Grady 1996: 98–109 *passim*.

21 Machiavelli's *The Prince* is clearly the *locus classicus* for a Renaissance linkage of instrumental rationality with autotelic political power, and as Marlowe suggested (as I read it) in *The Jew of Malta*, each of these themes is homologous to the self-perpetuating, corrosive and purposeless purposiveness of mercantile capitalism (Grady 1996: 26–33).

22 This pairing, I hope it is clear, is one of the reasons I insisted earlier in my discussion of Belsey's *Subject of Tragedy* (1985) on the need to differentiate an interior, libidinized subjectivity from an impersonal, objectifying instrumental rationality, rather than attempt, as Belsey did, to see each of these as a component of a unitary liberal humanism.

23 I am indebted to Eagleton 1986: 77 for an initial definition of this dynamic. See also on this topic Halpern 1991: 231–4.

4

We were never early modern
LINDA CHARNES

> The crisis in historicity now dictates a return, in a new way, to the question of temporal organization in general in the postmodern force field, and indeed, to the problem of the form that time, temporality, and the syntagmatic will be able to take in a culture increasingly dominated by space and spatial logic.
>
> (Jameson 1991: 25)

At a time when most Americans have never, arguably, been more ignorant about history, Shakespeare has never been more popular.[1] At first glance this seems like a paradox; but on closer view it presents not so much a contradiction as a mutually constitutive logic. For the recent upswing of mass cultural attention to Shakespeare is inseparable from a revival of popular interest in what I would call, for lack of a better term, 'the historical'. By 'the historical', however, I don't mean historiography as the art of writing events into the reified form we call 'history', but rather a philosophical 'structure of feeling': that certain *je ne sais quoi* that lets us postmoderns feel as if we're still living in a world marked by the passage of *meaningful time*. To understand Shakespeare's remarkable cachet in the late twentieth century, we must try to grasp what within our culture signifies 'historicity'. For whatever else Shakespeare may represent, he has come in the popular imaginary to stand for 'History itself'. But it is a history that has become increasingly 'apparitional' rather than narratological, synchronic rather than diachronic, affective rather than chronological, and aleatory rather than positivistic, a history that has come to function as an unarticulated national philosophy.

Of course, an apparitional Shakespeare is entirely appropriate in a culture that seeks 'the historical' not in narrative but in 'appearances' – in the figures of famous persons 'themselves'. A brief look at the 1992 film *Bill and Ted's Excellent Adventure* easily demonstrates this phenomenon. Bill and Ted are two middle-class high school seniors in (where else?) Southern California, on the verge of flunking out. Unless they can present a successful history project, Bill and Ted will not graduate from San Dimas High with their class.[2] Faced with this 'most heinous' possibility and knowing nothing about history, Bill and Ted manage to attract the help of ersatz-Olympian powers, who equip them with a time machine in the form of a telephone booth (complete with a Dialing-for-Destinies Directory).

All Bill and Ted have to do is let their fingers do the walking through the phone book of history: the machine carries them back to different periods and places, to the sides of the famous figures they ring up. Owing to serious time constraints and limited attention spans, Bill and Ted decide that instead of learning about history, they'll simply bring some historical 'dudes' back to the future with them, to appear on the high school stage as 'themselves' and therefore to present, by embodying, History. Since the standard American curriculum requires 'coverage', Bill and Ted round up Socrates, Genghis Khan, Billy the Kid, Napoleon, Joan of Arc, Beethoven, Freud and Lincoln. At the end of the film, their simultaneous presence in a musical extravaganza on the auditorium stage alludes to postmodernist history as pastiche: the way in which contemporary mass culture substitutes fantasies of hyperreal presence – what Baudrillard calls *Pataphysics*, a 'science of imaginary solutions' (1993: 149) – for the discursive processes through which a more 'traditional' ideology of history is formulated.

In other words, while Bill and Ted seem to choose their historical figures capriciously (and one wouldn't want to lean too hard on whatever crude principle of selection guides them), no choice that depends on instant name recognition can ever be truly random. However disjointed, these figures stand in the 'science of imaginary solutions' respectively for Wisdom (Socrates), Warrior Culture (Genghis Khan), the Wild West (Billy the Kid), Empire (Napoleon), Religious Zeal (Joan of Arc), Musical Genius (Beethoven), Modern Neurosis (Freud) and Freedom from Slavery (Lincoln). Aside from two token gestures towards multiculturalism (Genghis Khan) and gender (Joan of Arc), these historical figures – despite their apparent lack of connection – register, reductively to be sure, 'Western Civilization's' dialectical relationship between authoritarian conservatism and the maverick indices of its subversive (and specifically *Oedipally* subversive) or liberalizing modifications. Consequently, despite its pretensions to postmodern self-irony, the film's cultural intertext is neither post-ideological nor post-historicist. Legible within the film is a 'philosophy', however under-articulated, of history.

What kind of philosophy, then, does 'the historical' currently represent? Mass culture is being increasingly 'quilted', to use Lacan's term, by the *points de capiton* of what I would call the 'apparitional historical'. It is there-fore no accident that *Hamlet* is the play to which contemporary culture most frequently returns. Hamlet-the-Prince has come to stand for the dilemma of historicity itself. The play raises the hoary spectres that always haunt positivist narratives, and at once constitute, and interfere with, how stories achieve or lack advancement. As Terence Hawkes has argued, the structure of *Hamlet* is entirely recursive, a movement 'wholly at odds with the progressive, incremental ordering that a society, dominated perhaps by a pervasive metaphor of the production line, tends to think of as appropri-ate to art as to everything else' (Hawkes 1985: 312). Even within the Renaissance 'production line' of patrilineal inheritance and succession, the play fails:

> to run a satisfactorily linear, sequential course from a firmly established and well-defined beginning, through a clearly placed and signalled middle, to a causally related and logically determined end which, planted in the beginning, develops, or grows out of it.
>
> (312)

Forms of narratological production in *Hamlet* are always being derailed by apparitions, eruptions, symptomatic talkings-back, making the seemingly straightforward task of 'proper' rememoration impossible.

At stake here are two kinds of historical production: one narrative and the other apparitional, each of which generates entirely different experi-ences of time and representations of subjectivity. Within a Lacanian framework, the subject of narrative time is a non-subject, a dead letter; something that emerges as the reified Historical Figure. Such a figure is the by-product of what Bruno Latour calls 'calendar time'. As Latour puts it, 'Calendar time may well situate events with respect to a regulated series of dates'; but there is another kind of time that 'situates the same events with respect to their intensity' (Latour 1993: 68).

To situate the same events with respect to their intensity: this formulation sounds simple enough. But the subject of affective time is incommensurable with the order, and the nature, of *events*. This was one of Lacan's greatest insights, and one of his advances over Freud: his assertion that the true subject of the 'impossible real' isn't constituted by her narrative reconstruc-tion of her 'story' but rather by the *failure* of that story to 'include' its *affective* event-horizon – its epistemological starting- and end-point (Lacan 1991b: 86). As Joan Copjec has recently written about the Lacanian gaze:

> Where the Foucauldian and the film-theoretical positions always tend to trap the subject in representation (an idealist failing), to conceive of language as constructing the prison walls of the subject's being, Lacan argues that the subject sees these walls as *trompe l'œil*, and is thus constructed by something beyond them.
>
> For beyond everything that is displayed to the subject, the question is asked, 'What is being concealed from me? What in this graphic space does not show, does not stop *not* writing itself?'
>
> (Copjec 1994: 34)

This last question in Copjec's provocative passage bears repeating: What in this graphic space *does not stop not writing* itself? The double negative here figures absence as an active process of NOT WRITING, implying that there is something present that demands not to be written. Of course, Lacan, and Slavoj Žižek after him, would say that this impossible real is only posited retroactively to 'fill in' the trauma of originary absence: the 'real' as proleptic effect of what's always missing from representation.[3] As Copjec puts it:

> the veil of representation actually conceals nothing; there is nothing behind representation. Yet the fact that representation seems to hide [something] is not treated by Lacan as a simple error that the subject can undo . . . Rather, language's opacity is taken as the very cause of the subject's being, that is, its desire, or want-to-be. The fact that it is materially impossible to say the whole truth – that truth always backs away from language . . . founds the subject.
>
> (1994: 35)

On the one hand, this view certainly identifies the limits and even self-deceptions of most Foucauldian and Marxist-based ideology critique by pointing out their failure to comprehend the maverick role of desire in interpellation, the way desire often actively undermines ideology. On the other hand, Lacan's own form of anti-essentialism, evocative as it is, seems equally symptomatic of a similar denial, a specifically postmodern and (however inadvertent) ultimately cynical denial, of the subjective experience of historical incommensurability (Lacan 1991b: 58). Incommensurability is not the same as absence. But we can, and will, take this up later.

To not stop not writing is to engage in the ceaseless production of anti-chronicle, a non-representation of what's 'really going on' in calendar time. Thus we might say that for every chronicle there is a necessary anti-chronicle, for every reconstruction of calendrical events there is a condensation of significant intensities that cannot be intercalated into the resulting narrative. This isn't to say that 'affective time' achieves no representation. Rather, its representation is the specifically unwritten, undocumented, illegible. If calendar time records the progress of events as they appear in the registers of writing (with everything that implies about legal inscription within patrimonial culture), affective time seeks its representational truth in the non-narrativity of bodies.

Which brings us back to *Hamlet*. We can now note the way in which the significant intensities of the play guarantee that an accurate calendar-history of what actually 'happened' can never be produced. Despite Hamlet's charge to Horatio to tell the 'occurrents, more and less / Which have solicited' (V. ii. 362–3), Horatio has only been witness to a sequence of events. Whatever story he is able to tell will necessarily exclude Hamlet's *affective* history. This imperative to tell Hamlet's story – and its inevitable failure – generates the real legacy of the play. For we know that no adequate representation of affective time can ever make its appearance in Horatio's, or anyone else's, narrative of 'the play'. Thus we feel at the play's end all the future energy that will go into *the not writing of that story*, even as we know that *Hamlet* will, and has, become Western culture's paradigmatic narrative repetition compulsion.

No matter how many times we go back to *Hamlet*, we will never get it 'right', not because there's nothing there 'behind the scenes' but because the play lacks the one crucial element that would permit the narrative incorporation of affective time into calendar time: what Žižek calls the 'vanishing mediator'. As Žižek defines it (modifying Jameson's term), the vanishing mediator is:

> the structure of an element which, although nowhere actually present and as such inaccessible to our experience, nonetheless has to be retro-actively constructed, presupposed, if all other elements are to retain their consistency.
>
> (Žižek 1993: 33)

Unlike *Hamlet*, however, the *Henriad* does manage to provide just such a structure, with the 'clearly placed and signalled middle' occupied by 'the vanishing mediator'. In the *Henriad* the 'vanishing mediator' is the paternal metaphor and the symbolic logic of 'absolute monarchy'. This metaphor, a mere placeholder in the field of the Big Other, is that phantom to whom we all address the constitutive question, '*Che vuoi?*' or 'what is it that you want of me?' (Žižek 1989: 111–13). Providing the sanctified 'mandate' for the subject, its reason for 'answering the call', the place of the Big Other in early modern culture is occupied by God, Pope, King, Father, Lord – each of which quilts the paternal allegory over the 'fundamental antagonisms' of the social and calls things to order within it.

The *Henriad* charts the rise of a threat to the vanishing mediator, specifically the divine sanction of royal authority. In *Richard II*, the Big Other is simultaneously undercut and redeployed by Richard, who openly evinces contempt for 'fathers' (his treatment of Gaunt, for example) while believing he can retain the sanctification of Divine Right to secure his own position. But Richard puts too much faith in a conceptual category that unravels without the public investment of ideological belief in the signifier. Without such belief to bestow symbolic legitimacy on the 'sublime objects of ideology', there is nothing to mediate between potentially contestatory social, ideological and, in the *Henriad*, increasingly market-driven, forces.

Bolingbroke knows this, and will spend the rest of his dramatic life at least trying to resecure the branch he had simultaneously to saw off and stand on. If Richard's mistake was to take the doctrine of Divine Right too literally, Henry's is to put the paternal metaphor at risk by nakedly demonstrating how it too is subject to what Bataille calls the laws of homogeneous production (Bataille 1985: 140). Bolingbroke's usurpation has transformed the 'sacredness' of sovereignty (in Bataille's terms, its heterogeneous nature, its position outside the laws of 'normal' production) into just another market relation by too rapidly demystifying its operations, thus eliminating the necessary ideological mediation between forms of social commerce.[4] By failing to install another 'vanishing mediator' in the place of the royal paternal metaphor, Bolingbroke throws the status of the crown into ontological crisis.

This is the crisis that Hal inherits in *1 Henry IV*; and when the play opens he has retreated to the alternative, 'heterogeneous' ground of Eastcheap. During his sojourn in 'lad-culture', Hal substitutes for a time an 'other', obscene father, Falstaff, for a Father who cannot fully occupy the position of the Big Other. When Hal does finally renounce this 'second father', however, it won't be to return to the symbolic fold as Henry's son, but rather as Richard's son 'in spirit'.[5] Richard II will *retroactively* be installed as Hal's vanishing mediator, the mystifying element that will enable him to secure his own legitimacy within the symbolic order.

Consequently, there is in the *Henriad* (unlike in *Hamlet*) a positive recursiveness – a historically *productive* return of the repressed. The important point to be made here about the vanishing mediator is that even though it is 'vanishing', its presence as a subsumed structural element is crucial to the intelligibility of a social logic that can incorporate affective, as well as calendar, time. Without a vanishing mediator, no history – individual or collective – can be written. Which raises the question of what happens to the possibility of constructing a narrative history when the vanishing mediator is not replaced. Or more complicated yet, when we have multiple or competing mediators.

In *Hamlet* the Ghost is an excessively present 'obscene father': a 'father who knows'; and whose knowledge threatens the status of the symbolic mandate he imposes on his son.[6] The content of this knowledge consists not only of the 'harrowing' secrets of his purgatorial prison house, but more disturbingly, of the implied 'enjoyment' of the 'blossoms of his sin', for which he is, he tells Hamlet, 'confin'd to fast in fires, / Till the foul crimes done in my days of nature / Are burnt and purg'd away' (I. v. 11–13). At once delivering the paternal injunction to 'revenge' and revealing his own shadowy 'double', the Ghost commands Hamlet to 'remember me' even as he makes the task impossible, speaking the paternal mandate from a corrupted enunciatory site that splits the integrity of the Law open to reveal its kernel of obscene enjoyment. The second father emerges as a disturbance in the field of the Big Other, one that makes the mandates of identification impossible. This disturbance emerges as 'the obscene, uncanny, shadowy double of the Name of the Father' (Žižek 1992: 158). Unlike the traditional father, who guarantees the rule of Law by holding himself in neutral reserve, this other father is the embodiment of libidinal enjoyment, of the prurient pleasure that Lacan claims always underwrites phallocentric Law. This second father – which Žižek calls the Obscene Father – reveals the enjoyment that Law must disavow in order to retain its unquestionable shape.

Hamlet attempts to 'download' the obscene father into Claudius; but he cannot act on his knowledge of Claudius's guilt because, unable to assume the social existence that paternal identification would confer, Hamlet is literally incapable of finding his place in the story. And Claudius, like all good Derridean supplements, cannot contain everything he is supposed to 'hold'. The excess of paternal obscenity spills over onto everyone, including Ophelia and, most crucially, Gertrude. As long as the real obscene father hovers unacknowledged in the background, Gertrude takes on for Hamlet the character of 'traumatic Thing' – an Obscene Mother, if you will (Žižek 1992: 159–60). A grotesquely sexualized Gertrude becomes another vanishing mediator, another 'element which, although nowhere actually present and as such inaccessible to our experience, nevertheless has to be retroactively constructed, if all other elements are to retain their consistency'. We never see anything remotely resembling the lubricious Gertrude that the Ghost describes and Hamlet imagines; rather, as ideological supplement for the obscene father, she must be presupposed if we – and Hamlet – are to believe in the Ghost's tale of two 'adulterate beasts'.

Which isn't to say that the Ghost is lying; but the Ghost's revelation of his own obscene double puts the paternal mandate in doubt. If Hamlet 'lack[s] advancement' (III. ii. 331), it is because he is presented with several potential vanishing mediators at once, each of which represents a different historiographical possibility. Taken together, they stage the subjective destitution inflicted by an excess of historical *contingency*: by the possibility of competing, and therefore potentially self-cancelling, 'historemes' (Fineman 1989: 57). In other words, while we are accustomed to thinking of Hamlet's paralysis as the result of paternal overkill, symbolic *overdetermination*, I would suggest exactly the opposite: the problem is narrative *indeterminacy* brought about by the awareness of the radically contingent nature of rememoration – the fact that history can always be constructed in more ways than one, and therefore its truth is never to be located in a particular sequence of events.

Situating its 'hero' within the most positivist genre in the Renaissance (the revenge tragedy), the play proceeds to dismantle all linkage between causes and effects, generating instead of one deployable vanishing mediator a set of partial 'mediations' or monstrous 'hybrids'. Hamlet's task of piecing together the history of his 'family tree' is structurally, as well as chronologic-ally, interrupted by the choice of competing epistemologies. On what 'ground' does one build one's case? What is to be, or not to be, the 'matter' out of which historical knowledge can be assembled, or 're-membered'?

Some thirty years ago, Norman Rabkin argued that *Hamlet* is 'the para-digmatically Shakespearean' text insofar as it presents equally compelling yet incommensurable positions towards human experience. Foregrounding modern man's [*sic*] supreme faith in the powers of rationality, Rabkin argues, the play stages an equally compelling logic of the passions. Claiming that the play permits no bridging between these two modes of experience, Rabkin aligns Shakespearean 'greatness' with the 'insoluble' dilemma of modernity itself – which he characterizes as a division between the world of Reason, aligned with objectivity and 'Enlightenment', and the world of 'the passions', aligned with subjectivity and its libidinal irrationalities (Rabkin 1967: 4–7). However, if we push Rabkin's argument to contemporary conclusions, we might imagine that Hamlet would have fared better had Habermas, and not Horatio, been his friend. For while Horatio survives to 'tell Hamlet's story', it is a story that can only truthfully be told from within the gap *between* causes and effects – a space which Horatio's philosophy cannot cope withal. Hamlet's 'story', such as it is, takes place in the inter-stices of an intersubjectivity that the play always already debars. No one in this play 'knows' or 'understands' anyone else. Unequipped with a Habermasian lifeworld with which to negotiate modernity's supposed binary divisions, Hamlet's inability to build a narrative bridge between something represented as 'objective reality' and something presented as an 'excess of affect' is precisely what keeps calling him back to the contemporary cultural stage.[7]

The problem is not, as Francis Barker argued over a decade ago, that Hamlet is a 'modern' character ahead of his time, a prematurely Cartesian figure in an as yet undifferentiated social 'plenum' (Barker 1984), but that Hamlet is always already postmodern, or as Bruno Latour might put it, **amodern** – since one can't 'post' something that hasn't yet happened.[8] Hamlet's inability to 'be modern' remains the insoluble dilemma not only within the play but, I would argue, within contemporary mass culture as well. *Hamlet* keeps going, and going, and going, because the conditions for his reception STILL haven't arrived.

Hamlet occupies the incommensurable position of being *both harbinger of, and nostalgic signifier for*, what Latour calls 'the modern Constitution'. Latour explains that in the natural philosophy of the seventeenth century a 'division of power' arises between 'two protagonists': Robert Boyle, the inventor of the modern laboratory, with its capacity to engage in self-confirming and isolated experiments on 'real things' and thus establish their 'objective', or non-contextual, status, and Thomas Hobbes, creator of the discursive subject of the *Leviathan*, forever bound by the social authority of the political intertext. This division of knowledge and experience sets the stage for the great dramatic fiction of the modern Constitution, a tacit contract comprised of a set of assumptions and operations that 'invent a separation between the scientific power charged with representing things and the political power charged with representing subjects' (Latour 1993: 29). However, while this 'contract' acts as if it believes in the total ontological separation of objects and subjects, it 'simultaneously cancels out the separation' (37) through the resulting proliferation of *hybrids* in the space between the two poles. For in reality, as Latour argues:

> Everything happens in the middle, everything passes between the two, everything happens by way of mediation, translation, and networks, but *this space does not exist, it has no place. It is the unthinkable, the unconscious of the moderns.*
>
> (37, my emphasis)

Since modernity defines itself by the dual and mutually incompatible activities of 'purification' and 'mediation', its activities deny, even while fostering, the increasing production of 'hybrids': quasi-objects which cannot be cleanly located in the 'purified' realm of either the subject, or the object, poles of the modern Constitution.

What else is the Ghost in *Hamlet* but just such a hybrid, walking the 'unthinkable' realm between the separation of the object and subject poles? Presumably 'really there' in Act 1, its objective status is 'verified' by the fact that everyone present on the battlements sees it; however, later in III. iv., when Hamlet confronts Gertrude in her chamber, the Ghost's reality is thrown into ontological crisis by the fact that only Hamlet can see or hear it. What exactly *is* the status of this Thing? Is it really there or not? Surely it is meant, at least in Hamlet's mind, to function as a 'vanishing mediator', that element which 'although nowhere actually present . . . nonetheless has to be retroactively constructed, presupposed, if all other elements are to retain their consistency' (Žižek 1993: 33). But the Ghost, as monstrous hybrid or 'quasi-object' (Latour 1993: 51), fails to serve; what kind of 'father' is Hamlet supposed to 'remember'? Here the incommensurability of 'episteme' with 'historeme' is painfully obvious, and guarantees that Hamlet's charge to Horatio to tell 'the occurents, more and less / Which have solicited' (V. ii. 310) will never be realized.

The tenets, therefore, of so-called modernity cannot be maintained without the use of a 'vanishing mediator' to keep the divisions of experience in their respective places. Latour calls this mediator, which is at once *disavowed* and *held in reserve*, the 'Crossed-Out God' (1993: 32–3): a functionally 'sublime object' which can be called back into the picture whenever there are equally weighted ideological disputes between the object and subject poles. In the absurd position of having to keep issuing the call for such place-holders and evincing the proper degree of cynical distance, the modern Constitution is a self-cancelling proposition, established and maintained only by a fetishistic disavowal of its own conditions of impossibility.

As we are now (arguably) at the *fin de siècle* of the new historicist regime, and are besieged by the banalities of 'ever more minute refinements of the concept "postmodern"' (Bewes 1997: 47), perhaps the question we should be asking apropos of Hamlet's dilemma is not (with all due respect to Carolyn Porter) 'are we being historical yet?', but *are we being modern* yet? For it is precisely in the space of a *virtual modernity* that Shakespeare pitches Hamlet's tent. Hamlet, like any good 'slacker', is in search of a convincing reason to take up the paternal mandate; but of course, he can't find a convincing reason to act because this isn't really his job. Hamlet may lack advancement, but he doesn't lack employment: rather, his job is to walk the earth, for an uncertain term, pointing up modernity's failure to arrive. Poster boy for the nascent 'modern subject', Hamlet is also the death of the 'modern subject', if the Habermasian standard is the measure, by which the subject is a function of 'the principle of unlimited self-realization, the demand for authentic self-experience and the subjectivism of a hyperstimulated sensitivity' (Bewes 1997: 46). As Timothy Bewes puts it, '*of course the* subject is "dead" *and has always been so* if (a) the subject and (b) "living" are conceived in idealized, modernist-derived ways' (46). If Latour is correct, and I believe he is, in arguing that we have never been modern, then I would suggest that Hamlet has never been early modern, we have never been postmodern, and we are all, along with the pesky Prince, stuck in the same boat with regard to what, exactly, 'being historical' means.

In the face of such epistemological mortification, how are we to regard contemporary deployments of Shakespearean texts as guarantors of 'the historical' within the fiction of our own postmodern Constitution? We can approach this question by looking at a contemporary Shakespearean 'hybrid' that works with both the *Henriad* and, much less obviously, *Hamlet* – Gus Van Sant's 1992 film *My Own Private Idaho*. Van Sant's film takes the positivist 'storyline' of the *Henriad* and recasts it within an explicitly post-modernized framework. Young heir Scott Favor (played by an affectless Keanu Reeves, who also plays Ted in *Bill and Ted's Excellent Adventure*) disappoints his father, Mayor Jack Favor, by being 'an effeminate boy', living a sordid street life of male prostitution. He attaches himself to a surrogate father named Bob (referred to as the 'Fat Man') who recites many of Falstaff's lines throughout the film. Ultimately renouncing Fat Bob upon his father's death, Scott claims his inheritance, marries and returns to the bourgeois world. Despite the film's pretentiously 'postmodern' feel and its gestures towards pastiche and *unemplotment*, it clearly advances a chrono-logical telos of primogenitory movement towards a twenty-first birthday (the age of majority) and an inheritance of the father's place in the economic and, it is hinted, the political order.

Like Hal's inheritance of the crown, Scott's inheritance is guaranteed not by any actions of his own but merely by the passage of time. Unlike Hal, however, Scott's story is juxtaposed with another, *seemingly unrelated* tableau involving Scott's beloved and narcoleptic friend Mike (also a male hustler), and Mike's strange quest to find the elusive and ghostly mother of his childhood. While many critics have discussed the film's use of the *Henriad*, no one, to my knowledge, has noticed that encrypted within the film's *Henriadic Bildungsroman* is a strangely literalized and cross-gendered version of *Hamlet*. Although Scott's story will gain narrative ascendancy as the film progresses, *Private Idaho* begins, and ends, with Mike's dilemma. Haunted by shadowy memories of his mother and dreamlike scenes from his childhood, Mike suffers attacks of narcolepsy each time he tries to 'remember' her. His narcolepsy is an involuntary paralysis and loss of consciousness brought on by a 'hyperstimulated sensitivity', triggered each time he tries to put his past into some kind of narratological order – each time, in other words, he attempts to remember 'what really happened'.

Since Scotty Favor has nothing to do but 'kill time' until his twenty-first birthday, he decides to accompany Mike on his search for his mother. These two figures represent two different kinds of *historeme*, 'the smallest unit of historiographical fact' (Fineman 1989: 57). For Scotty, rememoration is unnecessary, since what drives his story is the automatic, chronological telos of patrimony. For Mike, however, the paternal metaphor has never been in place since, we discover, his biological father is actually his older brother, Richard (a literalization of the fratricidal incest motif in *Hamlet*). Rather, Mike's historeme is matrilinear: his Big Other is the Big Mother. Unlike Scott Favor, Mike's identity can't be secured by the symbolic logic of patrimonial (and patrinomial) inheritance. Instead, his identity depends upon the epistemological return to a specifically embodied origin. The maternal historeme is the body that matters. In *Private Idaho*, the absence of a living mother's body, and not the presence of a dead father's 'spirit', becomes the film's equally problematic 'vanishing mediator'.

While there seems to be little resemblance between Mike's subjective experience and Scotty's, there is a crucial connection – a Latourian 'middle' – that within the film at least must be disavowed in order for the *Henriadic* element to achieve its consistency. For however much calendar time situates events with respect to a series of dates, only affective time assigns meaning to the sense of 'history'. In Scotty's story, there is no mandate to carry out, since the paternal signifier is devoid both of affect and of content. For there to be any 'meaning' at all to Scott's story, he must derive it, parasitically, from Mike's. Providing the affective core of Scott's *Henriad* - its 'once more into the breach', as it were – Mike's *Hamlet*, with its 'excess of affect', fills out a narrative that has been reduced to the meaningless frame of calendar time.

In *Private Idaho*, both kinds of history – calendar time and affective time – are presented. 'Put together but kept separate', like Latour's description of the modern Constitution's project of purification and mediation, they lead to 'the ironic despair whose symptom is postmodernism' (Latour 1993: 67). Charting two kinds of movement, one an endless retracing of affective steps and the other a mere 'killing of time', the significant intensity of the former is sacrificed to the narrative logic of the latter. As the historical necessity of the *Henriad* gradually 'takes command' of the film, Mike's search for the missing Big Mother becomes an endless search for the 'ghost' of historical *meaning*. *Hamlet* remains, in the figure of Mike at the end of *Private Idaho*, to keep issuing the call for a history that discovers the affective truths held in, and delivered by, 'bodies that matter' (Butler 1993).

Clearly Hamlet and Hal, in whatever guise they take, have radically different 'destinies': one doomed forever to ride the road to nowhere, paralyzed ('Heaven and earth, must I remember?' I. ii. 143) by each onslaught of memory, and the other to ride effortlessly the progression of time to a preordained inheritance. The cynical ennui of the latter is 'filled in' by the significant intensity of the former. If every chronicle history is purchased by the *not writing* of another story, then the vanishing mediator doesn't really 'vanish' after all; rather, it retreats to the space between the subject/object poles, the place reserved for the 'Crossed-Out God', the place that breeds – in stubbornly non-modern fashion – epistemological hybrids. For the subject this represents the 'place between two deaths': the first symbolic and the second physical. As Žižek evocatively suggests, this is a place of sublime beauty as well as terrifying monsters:

> the site of *das Ding*, of the real-traumatic kernel in the midst of symbolic order. This place is opened by symbolization/historicization: the process of historicization implies an empty place, a non-historical kernel around which the symbolic network is articulated.
>
> (1989: 135)

However, while the 'place between two deaths' is opened up by symbolization/historicization, that place is never empty. When Žižek refers to the 'empty place of the Thing which enables us to conceive the possibility of a total, global annihilation of the signifier's network, the radical annihilation of nature's circular movement' (1989:135), what else is he doing but allegorizing in the realm of the subject the physics of the black hole – the singularity that radically annihilates everything around it not because it is empty but because its mass is so impossibly dense that nothing can escape its gravitational force? In the historical register we might say that as an object to be remembered achieves critical *affective* mass, it threatens to produce another kind of annihilation – a catastrophic sleep and a forgetting.

This is the real ghost of *Hamlet*. Not the Ghost of a murdered king but the spectre of a play that stands as the anti-chronicle to the *Henriad*, its proleptic condition of positivist possibility, its Crossed-Out God, stabilizing guarantor of the myth of the modern Constitution. In *Private Idaho*'s *Henriad manqué*, we see an elegy for a patriarchal legacy that can no longer be sustained by belief in the integrity of the Paternal Metaphor. In its place, we see a turn to the fantasy of maternal origin as a substitute for a Big Other that can no longer issue a believable interpellation. Tragically for Mike, the Big Mother is also nowhere to be found. Like Hamlet, Mike lacks a mediator that would enable him to suture his own subjectivity into a story that can actually *be told*. *Private Idaho* demonstrates that without the '*Che vuoi?*', without the belief that something more is required of the subject than the patrilineal mandate to 'redeem the time', there can only be subjective destitution – a historical narcolepsy that returns the 'unclaimed' subject, again and again, to the same road leading nowhere.

Which is precisely where Mike ends up. The film closes not with Scott

Favor's ascension into the place of the father, but with Mike's return to the same barren highway on which he began. The film's opening frame offers a definition of the word narcolepsy. Its final frame says 'Have a nice day'. We begin with unconsciousness and end with a mandate to *enjoy our time*. But it isn't historical time we are instructed to enjoy. In this evacuated equivalent of the paternal injunction, we hear the mandate delivered robotically by salesclerks and bank tellers, whose event horizons are determined by the daily rhythms of the Dow Jones – a world in which (like Scott Favor's) time is simply money, and nothing more. However 'affective' we might wish to suppose such a mandate is, it is no longer 'about' anything; its absence of both symbolic and libidinal 'matter' heralds the cynicism that makes it impossible to have a *meaningful* conversation 'with the dead'. 'Have a nice day' is the injunction that hails the arrival of virtual history.

Finally 'at issue is transference': the question of 'how an emotion come[s] to be displaced in its object' (Lacan 1991b: 226). I would like to conclude this chapter by making a hybrid claim, one that hovers 'in the middle' of the subject/object poles of psychoanalysis and historicism, the appropriate place, perhaps, of philosophy: the representation of calendar time carries a legacy composed of the 'indivisible remainder' that ghosts it. Every son who picks up the father's sceptre has a mortified double who wanders, forever asking the question, 'Now, mother, what's the matter?' (III. iv. 9). To say this is not to claim that women are the site of affective meaning, but to point out that in the kind of historiography that underwrites patriarchal culture, *whatever* is the 'not written' will constitute the Hamlet-effect. Every *Henriad* produces a *Hamlet* as its symptom.

The larger 'object' in question, to return to the road on which we began, is the figure of Shakespeare himself, into whom we have displaced our lost sense of 'the historical'. Contemporary fetishizing of Shakespeare enjoins a historical narcolepsy not unlike Mike's: one in which we attempt to locate ourselves as historical subjects by turning to a 'corpus' that we believe embodies our history for us. Like the Big Mother, Shakespeare offers the fantasy of a 'common' origin in which we might all 'find ourselves' represented. That we continue to demonstrate a cultural need for a body of *significant* intensity (as opposed to the empty intensities with which we are constantly bombarded by mass media) does not signal theoretical naivety, or nostalgia for a mythical 'centred subject', or a desire for the mappable contours of a 'modern' world. It does suggest, however, that Latour is correct when he says that 'postmodernism is a symptom, not a fresh solution' (1993: 46). Postmodernist critique is hobbled by the fact that:

> it lives under the modern Constitution, but it no longer believes in the guarantees the Constitution offers. It senses that something has gone

awry in the modern critique, but it is not able to do anything but prolong that critique, though without believing in its foundations.

(46)

And why is it unable to identify what 'has gone awry?' Because 'its adepts indeed sense that modernism is done for, but *they continue to accept its way of dividing up time*': its divisions of 'eras only in terms of successive revolutions' (46, my emphasis). As long as we continue to accept the modern Constitution's way of dividing up time, we will continue to operate inside its delusions; only now, we suffer as well from the 'cynical idealism' that results from demystifying a structure while still sitting comfortably within it. Bewes is correct to argue that: '[t]he reticence, the cautious historicism, and the political *self-limitation* of the post-structuralist (non-) critique are as complicit in this process as the "vulgarity" of a reified postmodernism' (1997: 48–9). At the same time, as long as we tolerate (and even celebrate), in the name of liberation from hegemonic narratives, a vision of postmodernism that refuses to 'produce connections between "things"' (Sloterdijk 1987: 313), contemporary culture can only be understood in terms of what Peter Sloterdijk calls 'the morality of journalists' and mass media: their proliferation not of hybrids, but of 'Ands' (313) – valueless juxtapositions of seemingly disconnected 'logical particles'. The danger Sloterdijk outlines is that 'in this indifference of the "And" vis-à-vis the things it places beside one another lies the germ of a cynical development' (313).

Meanwhile, the complexities of affective time will continue to proliferate in ways not mappable in terms of 'successive revolutions', revealing a fundamental incommensurability between subjectivity and historicity. To this extent, the very notion of a 'historicized subject' of early, mid- or postmodernity is a contradiction in terms. Perhaps this is one of the reasons why Shakespeare continues to be 'timeless': not because he 'transcends' History but because *we were never early modern*.

Coda

Several years ago scientists discovered, beneath a forest near Crystal Falls, Michigan, what they believe is the world's oldest and biggest living organism: a gigantic subterranean fungus. It weighs more than 100 tons, it's as big as ten football fields, and it is, they think, still growing. While scientists cannot actually see this Mother-of-all-Mushrooms, *they infer its existence* because, after running DNA tests on samples of tree mould taken from various places in the forest, they discovered that all of their samples were 'clones of the same genetic being': that what 'appeared on the surface as something familiar: button mushrooms on rotting wood . . . are just tips of a living iceberg spawned ages ago by a single spore'.[9] If we might for a moment think of contemporary mass culture as just such a forest of rotting wood, then we might speculate that the Shakespearean fragments and texts which are popping up all over its surface are not unlike 'button mushrooms': their presence reassuringly enables us to 'infer' that underneath all the historical 'debris', behind the fragmenting claims and postures of 'post-modernity', there is still 'a there there'; something – like the vanishing mediator – that we cannot actually see but whose presence must never-theless be posited for our cultural fantasies about ourselves to retain their consistency. Something Big. Something Other. Something that Matters. Something called Shakespeare.

Have a nice day.

Notes

1   Earlier versions of this essay were presented at the World Shakespeare Congress in Los Angeles, April 1996, and at SUNY Buffalo in November 1997. Michael D. Bristol has written extensively on Shakespeare's current marquis value in American mass culture: see *Big-time Shakespeare* (Bristol 1996: esp. 1–25).

2   Dimas is phonetically identical to *Demos*.

3   Slavoj Žižek 1989: esp. 55–62 describes the telemetry of ideological fantasy as a proleptic hermeneutic, the 'back to the future' effect of historical and psycho-analytic 'rememoration'.

4   In a chapter entitled 'The psychological structure of fascism', Bataille makes a distinction between two modes of 'the societal': the homogeneous and the het-erogeneous. *Homogeneous* society is productive, 'useful society', involving produc-tion that is always aimed at or for something else. *Heterogeneous* elements are those that are thought to exist 'for themselves', such as sacred or profane elements of mystical or seemingly 'non-productive' status (Bataille 1985: 137–49).

5   Paul Strohm 1996 has written a fascinating study of the symbolic resuscitation and redeployment of the 'real' Richard II in the early fifteenth century.

6   In Charnes 1997 I argue that Hamlet is the first *noir* text in Western literature, and Prince Hamlet the first *noir* detective/revenger. I then compare the treat-ments of the play in Franco Zeffirelli's 1990 film *Hamlet*, and Steve Martin's 1990 film *L.A. Story*.

7   The phrase 'excess of affect' with regard to Hamlet is, of course, T. S. Eliot's.

8   In anatomizing the contradictions between the theory and practice of the modern Constitution, Latour asserts:

> No one has ever been modern. Modernity has never begun. There has never been a modern world. The use of the past perfect tense is important here, for it is a matter of a retrospective sentiment, of a rereading of our history. I am not saying that we are entering a new era; on the contrary we no longer have to continue the headlong flight of the post-post-post-modernists; we are no longer obliged to cling to the avant-garde of the avant-garde; we no longer seek to be even cleverer, even more critical, even

deeper into the 'era of suspicion'. No, instead we discover that we have never begun to enter the modern era. Hence the hint of the ludicrous that always accompanies postmodern thinkers; they claim to come after a time that has not even started!

(1993: 47)

9 This story appeared in *The New York Times*, 5 April 1992.

5
Violence and philosophy:
Nathaniel Merriman,
A. W. Schlegel and Jack Cade

DAVID JOHNSON

I Introduction

The role of Shakespeare in the expansion of both the British and American empires has been the subject of critical reflection in recent years, and Western philosophy too has increasingly been read in colonial and neo-colonial frames. Of Shakespeare's global dissemination, for example, Ngugi wa Thiong'o concedes the power of *King Lear* and *Julius Caesar*, but nonetheless insists:

> The humanistic side of European literature reflects of course the democratic struggles of the European people. But given the domination of the West over the rest of the world through such repressive historical moments as the slave trade and slavery, colonialism and currently neo-colonialism, this literature tends to opt for silence or ambivalence or downright collaboration.
>
> (wa Thiong'o 1993: 14)[1]

And speaking of Western philosophy and colonialism, Howard Caygill captures the anxieties of this relation nicely:

> Is this world the 'realisation' of philosophy's universalist aspirations; is philosophy complicit with the European project of violent, imperial expansion; or is the course taken by world society nothing to do with the ideals of philosophy, at worst their grotesque perversion?
>
> (Caygill 1993: 48)[2]

This chapter continues with these uncomfortable questions by focusing upon a particular fragment of colonial history, which combines in compressed form elements of Shakespeare, Western philosophy and colonial violence. I examine a lecture by Archdeacon Nathaniel Merriman entitled *Shakespeare as Bearing on English History*, and delivered on behalf of the General Institute of Grahamstown in the Eastern Cape in 1858. In considering Merriman's lecture, I focus on three elements: Merriman's reading of Jack Cade's rebellion in *2 Henry VI* (Shakespeare); his extensive reliance upon A. W. Schlegel's *Course of Lectures on Dramatic Art and Literature* (philosophy); and his relation to the wars of conquest waged by the British in the Eastern Cape against the Khoi and the Xhosa in the 1850s (colonial violence). In conclusion, I suggest that traces of Schlegel and Merriman's Shakespeare reverberate in contemporary Shakespeare criticism.

II Nathaniel Merriman

Born on 4 April 1809 in Wiltshire, Nathaniel James Merriman was educated at Winchester College and Brasenose College, Oxford.[3] He was ordained in 1835, married Julia Potter in 1840, and the same year was appointed curate of the Somerset village of Street. During the next five years, they had five children, and in 1848, the family moved to the Cape Colony, where Merriman took up the position of Archdeacon of Grahamstown, with the task of supervising the Anglican Church in the Eastern Cape. In the Grahamstown of the 1850s, Merriman was a controversial figure for at least two reasons: first, he favoured the Tractarian 'High Church' views associated with Dr E. B. Pusey in an environment where the opposing Evangelical position held sway; and second, he showed what one commentator has called 'a natural aptitude for simple living' (Varley and Matthew 1957: xii), which meant that he eschewed the decorum associated with his position, and walked vast distances (up to forty miles a day) in ministering to the needs of his parish. He kept detailed journals of his journeys between November 1848 and August 1855, with the entries between 1850 and 1852 edited by Bishop Robert Gray of Cape Town and published by George Bell in London in 1853 as *The Kafir, the Hottentot and the Frontier Farmer*. In the later part of the decade, Merriman turned his hand to Shakespeare, delivering in 1857 a lecture on behalf of the General Institute of Grahamstown entitled *On the Study of Shakespeare*, and in 1858, he delivered the lecture on *Shakespeare as Bearing on English History*.

The Grahamstown of the 1850s had a developed public sphere, with two newspapers – the *Grahamstown Journal* and the *Anglo-African* – and several learned societies, which included the General Institute (associated with the Anglican Church), the Albany Society (connected with the Wesleyan

Church) and the Literary and Scientific Society.[4] These societies offered public lectures, and often competed fiercely for audiences. In 'Notes of the week', the *Grahamstown Journal* of 26 April 1856, for example, reports on four lectures that had taken place the preceding week: on the Wednesday, a mathematics lecture on notation signs by Mr Tudhope; on the Thursday, a very crowded lecture on the geology of the Cape by Mr A. G. Bain under the auspices of the Literary and Scientific Society; and on the Friday, two lectures, one by Bishop Armstrong on Oliver Goldsmith's poetry organized by the General Institute, and one by the Revd R. Lamplough on geology and 'the harmonious relation this science bore to the Sacred Scriptures' (4) organized by the Albany Institute. Merriman's first lecture *On the Study of Shakespeare* was delivered in the first week of September 1857, and was a great success. The 'Colonial extracts' column in the *Anglo-African* of 3 September 1857 reports that there were more than 450 persons present, and many more who could not gain admittance, and the 'Notes of the week' in the *Grahamstown Journal* of 5 September 1857 records how the Lord Bishop in his vote of thanks requested on behalf of the delighted audience that the lecture be printed. Responding to public demand, Merriman then delivered his second lecture on Shakespeare and the history plays on Friday, 6 November 1857. Again, the lecture was well attended, and Merriman did not disappoint: 'Notes of the week' of 7 November 1857 describes the audience as 'large and deeply interested' (4), and 'Colonial extracts' of 12 November 1857 enthuses that the second lecture was 'admirably conceived, beautifully written, and delivered in that fine manly tone which must attest and fix the attention' (4). As was the custom, the evening concluded with music by a local military band, and the singing of the national anthem.

Merriman opens this second lecture by insisting upon the importance of protecting and promoting Shakespeare in Grahamstown:

> The subject [of the lecture] should be interesting to us, for the History and poetry alike of our mother land is the common inheritance of us all. An inheritance so much the more precious to those who dwell in a distant Colony, as without any proper History or Native Literature of our own, we should but for this, be cut off from some of the most ennobling associations which belong to the cherished name of Englishman.
>
> (Merriman 1858: 1)

The first-person pronouns here suggest a white English settler audience anxious about losing touch with England. Familial and legal metaphors overlap as Merriman confronts the fear of being 'cut off from . . . the common inheritance . . . of our mother land'. His remedy? Stay in close touch with Shakespeare.

Merriman's first assumption – with extensively cited support from Archbishop Whately, A. W. Schlegel, Henry Reed and Coleridge – is that history is much more than a list of dates and facts. Imagination is essential to the study of history: 'he who does not bring an active and cultivated imagination to bear upon what he reads, will certainly miss the noblest ends to which the uses of Historical knowledge can be applied' (2). For Merriman, Walter Scott demonstrates the value of imagination brilliantly in his novel *Ivanhoe*, a fact happily conceded by French historian of the Norman Conquest, Thierry. However, it is Shakespeare more than anyone who demonstrates how the imagination can reconfigure history to the 'noblest ends'.

What then are these 'noblest ends'? Merriman offers two related proposals. The first is implied in the opening appeal to the 'cherished name of Englishman'. Referring to the historical liberties Shakespeare takes with the official chronicles in his plays *Henry V* and *King John*, Merriman notes that '[i]t was however the Poet's purpose at the close of either play, to leave a favourable impression of the hopefulness of the political estate of England' (5). This is seen as quite in order, given that the plays were written while Shakespeare was experiencing 'a glow of patriotic enthusiasm, on witnessing the trophies from the defeat of the Spanish Armada' (5). In other words, for Merriman, history can be imaginatively rearranged to serve the nation.

The second noble end served by the imagination's adjusting of history is the service of God. Surveying with some contempt 'Hume's sneering' (6) and 'Macaulay's irreligious vein' (7), Merriman warmly approves Schlegel and Arnold's religious spirit. Describing 'the high function of dramatic art [as] exhibiting God's Providence, and the laws of the moral universe' (5), Merriman concludes:

> [T]he studious shutting out from our sight of the overruling hand of a Divine Providence, which marks some of our modern historians, is a far more pernicious obstacle to a correct view of history than any mistaken chronology into which we might fall from the studies of Shakespeare's dramas.
>
> (6)

Examples of Shakespeare's sure religious sense are provided first in *1 Henry IV*, where the hero makes respectful mention of the Crusades – for Merriman, '[o]ur recent sad lessons in India [show] what the true spirit of unchecked Mahomedanism is' (6)[5] – and second, in his 'religious representation of the reign of Henry V' (7).

While Merriman recognizes Shakespeare's interested use of historical sources in *King John, 1 & 2 Henry IV, Henry V* and *Richard III* to serve national security and God's Providence, in his reading of *2 Henry VI*, he sees no such imaginative deviation from the historical records. Rather, what he sees in *2 Henry VI* is a demonstration of Shakespeare's great skill in dramatizing historical 'truths' of eternal validity. The first such truth is the role of the monarchy in furthering 'the Progress of Education, – the Liberty of the Press, and the Establishment of Schools' (14). Conceding that 'these are commonly represented as though they were in earlier times (what they are now) popular movements' (14), he insists that in the time of Henry VI, efforts for popular education came from above: 'as they [the people] rose from feudal servitude, schools in London and throughout the realm were extensively endowed. In this, as we know, the King himself took the lead' (14). What clinches this argument for Merriman is Jack Cade's violent hostility in the play towards all who could read: unequivocal proof that 'the work of the wealthy and the noble in promoting learning' (14) was rejected by the people. Henry VI's commitment to education is further celebrated in the closing paragraph of the lecture, where Merriman notes that Henry founded Eton College. Merriman quotes at length the Bishop of Lincoln praising Henry for this deed:

> Yet it has pleased the Almighty to ordain that this despised, this suffering monarch should exercise a more powerful influence over the future ages than many princes whose exploits are the theme of the world's applause . . . To the intellectual and moral training to which the youthful mind is here subjected, is perhaps owing more than to any other single cause, the formation of that national character, which has under the Divine blessing, raised England to its eminent position among the peoples of the earth.
>
> (16)

Despite his failure to transcend the painful agonies of the Wars of the Roses, Henry VI therefore bequeathed to the English nation a precious check against the likes of Cade: the ideal of an education system along the lines of Eton.

The second uncontroversial truth Merriman uncovers in *2 Henry VI* is that revolutionary violence is an unqualified evil. He refers again to Schlegel in reaching this conclusion:

> His [Cade's] mode of putting Lord Saye and his son-in-law to death is no less characteristic, so that Schlegel writing close upon the French Revolution, and remembering doubtless how the revolutionary Tribunal had condemned with ferocity all that had any pretensions to literary,

scientific, or even artistic fame, says – 'Shakespeare had delineated the conduct of a popular demagogue, and the fearful ludicrousness of an anarchical tumult of the people, with such convincing truth that one would believe him to have been eye-witness of many of the events of our age; which, from ignorance of history have been considered without example.' . . . [The Terror] is but a counterpart to much that Shakespeare had (no doubt with traditionary correctness) ascribed three centuries before to Cade. But as a relief to the horrors of war the Dramatist could afford to throw around it what Schlegel truly calls a 'fearful ludicrousness'.

(15)

For Merriman, what Shakespeare therefore provides in reworking English history in his plays of the 1590s is a powerful set of moral injunctions: serve the nation; obey God; pursue a public school education; and beware revolutionary violence!

III Philosophy

At several key moments in his lecture on Shakespeare's history plays, Merriman shores up his arguments with reference to A. W. Schlegel's *Lectures on Dramatic Art and Literature*. In expanding upon these moments of influence, I also emphasize certain of Schlegel's arguments ignored or modified by Merriman.

Schlegel's *Lectures on Dramatic Art and Literature* was based on lectures organized by his patron, Madame de Staël, and delivered by him in Vienna in 1808. De Staël had been banished from France by Napoleon in 1804, and in Berlin in that same year had employed Schlegel as tutor to her children. After several years at Coppet on Lake Geneva, she and Schlegel arrived in Vienna in the autumn of 1807, where she set about promoting his lectures. Schlegel in the Preface to the *Lectures* recalls the occasion with breathless affection:

I delivered these Lectures, in the Spring of 1808, at Vienna, to a brilliant audience of nearly three hundred individuals of both sexes . . . I found here the cordiality of better times united with that amiable animation of the South, which is often denied to our German seriousness, and the universal diffusion of keen taste for intellectual amusement . . . [I lay] my gratitude at the feet of the benignant monarch who, in the permission to give these Lectures communicated to me by way of a distinction immediately from his own hand, gave me an honourable testimony of his gracious confidence . . . [At the end of the Lectures], a general emotion was perceptible, excited by so much that I could not say, but respecting which our hearts understood each other.

(Schlegel 1846: 5)

Not everyone remembered the lectures quite so warmly: literary historian Thomas Sauer observes that '[t]he few extant references to them [the lectures] from members of the audience, however, indicate dissatisfaction – with Schlegel's delivery and content and with the hall itself in which a band of cats roamed among the audience's legs during the lectures' (Sauer 1981: 27). Even though the lectures did little more than synthesize Schlegel's earlier work (itself heavily indebted to the more original minds of fellow Romantics associated with the *Athenaeum*), they were greeted with great enthusiasm upon being published in 1811. Two more editions were published in German before 1841, and they were swiftly translated into all the major European languages, with English editions in 1815 and 1846. Merriman's reliance on Schlegel is testimony to the extent of his influence, though it should be added that other German Romantics were also read with close interest by the literati at the Cape, without necessarily first being routed through the English Romantics.[6]

The first of Schlegel's ideas taken up by Merriman is the perception of Shakespeare as supreme English genius. For Schlegel, there are several good reasons for elevating Shakespeare. Most obviously, Shakespeare represents for Schlegel the pre-eminent instance of the modern genius, who confounds the aesthetic categories of classical antiquity. This polemical context dictates therefore that Schlegel puts forward Shakespeare principally to refute the conservative defenders of classical critical standards:

But no man can be a true critic or connoisseur without universality of mind, without that flexibility which enables him, by renouncing all personal predilections and blind habits, to adapt himself to the peculiarities of other ages and nations . . . There is no monopoly of poetry for particular ages and nations; and consequently that despotism in taste, which would seek to invest with universal authority the rules which at first, perhaps, were but arbitrarily advanced, is but a vain and empty pretension. Poetry, taken in its widest acceptation, as the power of creating what is beautiful, and representing to the eye and ear, is a universal gift of Heaven, being shared to a certain extent even by those whom we call barbarians and savages. Internal excellence is alone decisive, and where this exists, we must not allow ourselves to be repelled by the external appearance.

(Schlegel 1846: 18–19)

The ambiguous radicalism of German Romanticism, which attracted subsequent thinkers like Walter Benjamin, is evident in this passage. On the one hand, Schlegel rejects the inflexible criteria of classical criticism, and (theoretically, at least) recognizes the relative value of different nations and their literatures. On the other hand, he transfers value to writers of genius like Shakespeare, whose 'internal excellence is alone decisive' in establishing their superior worth.[7] For Merriman, it is only the latter which carries weight: he has no sense of his Shakespeare criticism combating a conservative critical orthodoxy, and as far as he is concerned, neither the settler communities nor the indigenous nations of the Cape 'have [a] History or Native Literature of their own' (Merriman 1858: 1).

In addition to defying the tyranny of classical critical standards, Shakespeare's relation to England for Schlegel represents an ideal to be envied: 'Shakespeare is the pride of his nation. A late poet has, with propriety, called him "the genius of the British isles"' (Schlegel 1846: 345). Denouncing critics of Shakespeare like Voltaire, who described Shakespeare's plays as the '"work of a drunken savage"' (348), and Hume, who suggested that 'a reasonable propriety of thought [Shakespeare] cannot for any time uphold' (348), Schlegel declares that 'he appears a profound artist' who has 'deeply reflected on character and passion, on the progress of human events and destinies, on the human constitution, on all the things and relations of the world' (358–9). His only regret, and it is one he turns to in his final lecture, is that Shakespeare was not German. Bemoaning the fragmented state of the German people – 'we Germans . . . formerly the greatest and most illustrious nation of Europe . . . are in danger of disappearing altogether from the list of independent nations' (529) – Schlegel cites great moments in German history, and cries out for a literary genius to reconstruct them in ways that might promote national unity: 'What a field for a poet, who, like Shakespeare, could discern the poetical aspect of the great events of the world' (538). In much the same way as the Romantic critics like Coleridge and Hazlitt, Merriman happily accepts the German applause for Shakespeare. In the process, Shakespeare is transformed from an object of German envy to a subject of English national pride, or in Merriman's case, of English imperial authority.

The third of Schlegel's ideas taken up by Merriman relates to Shakespeare's use of history. Still concerned to defend Shakespeare from the criticism of 'a learned and critical, but by no means poetical age' (357), Schlegel insists that Shakespeare was fortunate to have had only the chronicles to rely on for his history plays:

[T]he history of his own country was familiar to him in every detail. Fortunately for him it had not as yet been treated in a diplomatic and pragmatic spirit, but merely in the chronicle-style; in other words, it had not yet assumed the appearance of dry investigations respecting the development of political relations, diplomatic negotiations, finances, &c., but exhibited a visible image of the life and movement of an age prolific of great deeds.

(355)

As with his promotion of Shakespeare as a 'modern' genius, Schlegel's defence of Shakespeare's use of history occurs in a polemical context, with Schlegel concerned to score points against increasingly influential empiricist historical methods. Against the pedantry of 'objective' history, Schlegel offers the imagination of a poetic history: 'Of every historical transaction Shakespeare knows how to seize the true poetical point of view, and to give unity and rounding to a series of events detached from the immeasurable extent of history without in any degree changing them' (414). He elaborates the advantages of Shakespeare's method in his English history plays:

> The principal features of the events are exhibited with such fidelity; their causes, and even their secret springs, are placed in such a clear light, that we attain from them a knowledge of history in all its truth, while the living picture makes an impression on the imagination which can never be effaced.

(419)

Merriman agrees in close detail with Schlegel's arguments here about Shakespeare's use of history, but Schlegel emphasizes a slightly different reason for Shakespeare's creative licence with the past. Lecturing in Vienna in 1808, Schlegel reveals a continuing sympathy for monarchical forms of governance, as he argues that Shakespeare's chief end in rewriting history was to '[furnish] examples of the political course of the world, applicable to all times' (420). In particular, he stresses the educative value of the plays for feudal rulers:

> This mirror of kings should be the manual of young princes; from it they may learn the intrinsic dignity of their hereditary vocation, but they may also learn from it the difficulties of their situation, the dangers of usurpation, the inevitable fall of tyranny, which buries itself under its attempts to obtain a firmer foundation; lastly, the ruinous consequences of the weaknesses, errors, and crimes of kings, for whole nations, and many subsequent generations.

(420)

Fifty years later, and writing in a British colony, Merriman in his

Shakespeare criticism ignores Schlegel's nostalgia for a benevolent feudal paternalism, and emphasizes rather Shakespeare's ability in the history plays to dramatize God's Providence, and/or celebrate the (British) nation.

The fourth idea of Schlegel approved by Merriman is implicit in the former's affection for wise princes practising their hereditary vocation, namely his fear of violent revolution. It is a commonplace that the early German Romantics initially embraced the French Revolution, but turned against it with the Terror and the rise of Napoleon.[8] As late as 1796, August Wilhelm's younger and more radical brother Friedrich was still writing that '[i]nsurrection is not politically impossible or absolutely illegitimate' (Schlegel 1996: 111), and specifying two situations in which insurrection is justified: first, when the motive of the insurrection is 'destruction of the constitution [and] whose goal is the organization of republicanism' (111–12); and second, when there is the 'existence of an *absolute* despotism [which is] an incomparably greater evil than *anarchy*' (112). However, by the start of the nineteenth century, such sentiments had to a greater or lesser degree with all the German Romantics been replaced by a deep hostility towards popular revolution. August Wilhelm's fear of revolution in *Lectures on Dramatic Art and Literature* is of course most clearly expressed in Schlegel's identification of Jack Cade's rebellion in *2 Henry VI* with the violence of the French Revolution: the 'popular demagogue' Jack Cade, and the 'fearful ludicrousness of the anarchical tumult of the people' (434) might for Schlegel as easily have served as portraits of Robespierre and the Paris mob. Schlegel is consoled though by the thought that '[b]loody revolutions and devastations of civil war appear . . . as a relapse into an earlier and more uncultivated condition of society' (438), and that Shakespeare's history plays accurately reflect the gradual progress from 'the powerful confusion of the middle ages, to the regular tameness of modern times' (439). In other words, violent civil discord, from the Wars of the Roses to the French Revolution, is gradually being superseded by more prosaic, but less savage rhythms of social progress. Again in this instance, Merriman modifies Schlegel's arguments slightly, agreeing entirely with him regarding the undesirability of violent rebellion, but unable to share his optimism regarding an inexorable historical progression away from civil wars and revolutionary violence.

IV Colonial violence

Merriman's lectures on Shakespeare might be read as unremarkable Victorian bardolatry, substantially bolstered by the arguments of A. W. Schlegel. However, Merriman's context suggests the need for a more complicated reading, as Schlegel's ideas about Shakespeare in Vienna in 1808 assume new meanings when repeated in Grahamstown in 1857.

The Eastern Cape frontier in the 1850s, and Grahamstown in particular, was at the centre of devastating colonial wars between the English and both the Khoi and the Xhosa. These included: the Kat River Rebellion of 1851, where the colonial government crushed an uprising of the Christian Khoi, and transferred their land to white farmers; the War of Mlanjeni of 1850–3 between the Xhosa and Sir Harry Smith's colonial troops, described by historian Jeff Peires as 'the longest, hardest and ugliest war ever fought over one hundred years of bloodshed on the Cape Colony's eastern frontier' (Peires 1989: 12); and the Cattle-Killing of 1856–7, and its genocidal aftermath orchestrated by Governor George Grey, which saw 35,000–40,000 Xhosa dead, 150,000 more Xhosa displaced, and 600,000 acres of Xhosa land passing into the hands of white farmers. At the time of Merriman's two Shakespeare lectures, white Grahamstown was faced with thousands of starving Xhosa seeking food and shelter in their town. With government policy under Grey effectively directed to starving the Xhosa into submission, Christian charity in Grahamstown was carefully measured, as the 'Colonial extracts' column of the *Anglo-African* of 3 September 1857 reflects:

> What are we going to do with the starving Kaffirs? ... When exhaustion and debility shall have made room for repletion and brawny strength, the aggressive propensities and confused ideas about *meum* and *teum* of these children of nature may convert these helpless objects of charity into sturdy beggars; and, unless it can be proved that gratitude is among the virtues of savages, we may find their immediate proximity not very favourable to our comfort and security.
>
> (2)

Merriman's writings of the period show him grappling with these contradictions, expressing attitudes ranging from fear and anxiety, to a defensive desire for racial and social order.

In trying to understand resistance to the colonial order, Merriman not surprisingly reaches for English antecedents. Reflecting in August 1851 upon the Kat River Rebellion, Merriman observes:

> It is a very remarkable circumstance, that the teaching of the Independents appears to have produced in this land a re-enactment of those very scenes which were the fruit of their predominance in England two hundred years since: viz. as the Prayer Book expresses it, 'the turning of religion into rebellion, and faith into faction.' Our rebels, like Cromwell's soldiers or worse, read their Bibles, pray, and even

receive Holy Communion to-day when they are going to dedicate the
morrow to rebellion and wayside murder.

(Varley and Matthew 1957: 155)

A month later, on 28 September 1851, Merriman records an awkward
conversation with Dr John Philip's wife, where he again reaches for an
English analogy to explain tensions between the settlers and the local
inhabitants:

> I was pained by the unEnglish and bitter spirit which Mrs Philip and
> the other missionaries resident with them evinced in their conversation.
> In their eyes colonization seems to be a sin . . . I felt very much hurt at
> this sort of discourse, especially when the missionary began ranting
> about 'our grasping at land in the Sovereignty', which is an arrant
> fiction, I believe. If the European population could but live peaceably
> on their lands without being plundered by their black neighbours, they
> would have small wish to extend the Colonial Territory. But if an
> English farmer finds his lands surrounded by marauding and pilfering
> gipsies, he will naturally wish to remove the nuisance by ejectment, by
> purchase of neighbouring fields, or in any other way that he best can,
> and the same law holds good in South Africa.
>
> (Varley and Matthew 1957: 159)

In both these passages, Merriman is confronted with challenges to his
notion of social order: the Khoi rebels – like Cromwell's Puritans –
reinterpret the Scriptures in defying the colonial regime's political order,
and African farmers – like pilfering gipsies – ignore the 'property rights' of
white farmers. In both instances, Merriman endorses, if in euphemistic
terms, recourse to military violence to restore order.

There are moments when the extreme harshness of military policy on the
Frontier sees him moderating somewhat his allegiance to order.[9] After a visit
to Sarhili (referred to as Kreli by Merriman) in July 1855, for example, he
encounters *en route* back to Queenstown surviving fugitives from the Kat
River Rebellion, and the spectacle of their desperation evokes some
compassion:

> On the whole I felt much pity for them and grieved again at what I
> thought the mistaken leniency which prevented the Government from
> making at once an example of some 5 or 6 of the leaders of the
> rebellion who were taken after the capture of Fort Armstrong in the
> Kat River Settlement. Had this been done it seemed to me these poor
> fellows, originally some 500 in number, might have been safely

pardoned after the War instead of being hunted into the bush as they now are, being afraid to shew their faces anywhere in the colony for fear of the consequences.

(Varley and Matthew 1957: 225)

Yet Merriman still does not question the legitimacy of colonial governance; rather, he disagrees with the particular coercive strategies used (expropriation of land), and suggests instead punishment along the lines of that meted out to Jack Cade: make a vivid example in punishing the leaders of the rebellion, and the intimidated followers will then be incorporated as meek subjects into the colonial order.

Merriman's commitment to order was not limited to the order of the colonial regime. He also revealed a respect for the authority structures of African societies. In recalling his meeting near Butterworth with Sarhili, Merriman declares his respect for the authority of the chief over his own people. In terms which anticipate the arguments of Lord Lugard for indirect rule, Merriman explains his efforts to secure a missionary settlement as near to the chief's capital as possible as follows:

I urged [Sarhili] that it was himself and his counsellors whom we were anxious to teach. Moreover, that we wished to teach his people obedience to their chief as part of the doctrine of God's word, and if we settled far off discontented and turbulent subjects would come to us setting their chief's authority at defiance and how were we to prevent this?

(Varley and Matthew 1957: 223)

What Merriman explicitly opposes here then is not independent African authority, but rather those 'discontented and turbulent subjects', who might defy the order established by the chief.

Although they are written several years before his Shakespeare lectures, these journals reveal that Merriman's reading of the colonial landscape shares much with his reading of Shakespeare's dramatic landscape. In Shakespeare, God's Providence is on the side of monarchy and social order (even if they are represented by weak kings like Henry VI), and is resolutely against seditious types like Jack Cade. On the East Cape frontier, right is on the side of social order as represented most prominently by the colonial government and its law, but also by the chiefly authorities like Sarhili. Threats to this order – less easily dealt with than Jack Cade in *2 Henry VI* – include rebellious Khoi Christians, African farmers indifferent to the property claims of white farmers, and Africans outside the jurisdiction of traditional leaders.

How then do the meanings of Merriman and Schlegel's critical assumptions – that Shakespeare is a modern English genius; that Shakespeare's imagination is the guide to true history; and that Shakespeare dramatizes the evils of popular rebellion – change in travelling from Vienna in 1808 to Grahamstown in 1857? Schlegel's arguments were staged within an expanding German-speaking public sphere in Europe, and as a result, his promotion of Shakespeare means something like: 'As educated Germans, we must appreciate England's literary genius, and hope that our own troubled nation soon produces a similarly luminous figure.' Merriman, on the other hand, writes within an English colonial public sphere, and his pronouncements on Shakespeare mean something like: 'As isolated English settlers, we must appreciate our greatest literary hero, and promote both him and England's interests among the lower races of the Colony.' In other words, the same arguments in Schlegel's lecture which connote a longing on the part of one (weaker) European power to emulate another (more powerful) European power, in Merriman connote a monological cultural imperialism.

V Jack Cade

Having looked at Jack Cade's fate in a colonial context, how might we now read him in a neo-colonial context? Recent Anglo-American Shakespeare criticism suggests at least two possibilities, both of which reveal strong continuities with the ideas of Schlegel and Merriman.

The first reading of Cade is provided by Annabel Patterson, an American critic writing in the late 1980s. Like Merriman, Patterson announces a keen appreciation of the 'sacredness of Shakespeare's power' (Patterson 1989: 162). Unlike Merriman, however, Patterson is concerned to demonstrate a sensitivity on Shakespeare's part to the poorer classes, and she rejects firmly any notion of Shakespeare as an apologist for the rich.[10] For her, the truth about Shakespeare is more complicated: in *2 Henry VI*, Gloucester, she argues, provides 'the genuinely popular leadership . . . of which the commons are now deprived' (48), and in Gloucester's absence, Salisbury functions as a temporary 'people's spokesman' (48). The sympathetic portrayal of these two characters and their efforts on behalf of the poor prompts Patterson to conclude that Shakespeare does indeed give 'conditional approval of the role of popular protest in the play – conditional, that is, on rightful motives, a basic loyalty to the crown, and a proper spokesman' (48). As for Cade, he 'fails every test for the proper popular spokesman' (48), and accordingly represents the wrong kind of populism. The difference between Gloucester and Cade is then summed up as follows: 'Shakespeare's own intentions have already been indicated by his dramatizing different styles of populism, by distinguishing between authoritative [Gloucester] and specious [Cade] mediation of popular goals and grievances' (50). She repeats this distinction in another way on the next page, where she argues that Shakespeare discriminates between 'socially useful or abusive styles of its mediation' (51). This complexity in the text ultimately means then that 'there is nothing in *Henry VI, Part 2*, read carefully, that can justify its use as the court of last appeal in a claim for Shakespeare's conservatism' (51).

Seen in the context of the USA in the late 1980s, Patterson's Cade – guilty of 'specious' and 'abusive' styles of mediation (*not* rebellion) – suggests a *Time* magazine version of Mumid Abu-Jamal's confrontation with the American state. For Patterson, legitimate violence is the exclusive preserve of the state, and the approved – 'authoritative' or 'socially useful' – means of registering popular protest would presumably be to lobby the Democratic Party, or (more recklessly) contact Jesse Jackson's rainbow coalition.

A second possible reading of Jack Cade is the one offered by Richard Wilson, a British materialist critic. Wilson agrees with Merriman that Shakespeare contributes to the defence of ruling-class interests by writing Cade as despicable villain, but whereas Merriman applauds Shakespeare for doing so, Wilson attacks this 'character assassination' (Wilson 1986: 170) of Cade. After careful historical investigation, Wilson explains the depiction of Cade as rooted in Shakespeare's own (economic) investment in the suppression of the cloth workers' struggles of the 1590s. Wilson argues:

> With his gruesome 'slaughter house' of victims and plot to rape the burghers' wives, Shakespeare's Cade is a projection of the sexual and cannibalistic terrors of the Renaissance rich. The scenes in which he figures should be interpreted as a self-interested intervention by the management of The Rose in London's crisis, and a cynical exploitation of atavistic fears.
>
> (1986: 176)

Wilson concludes by pointing to the continuities from the original Globe to the rebuilding of the Globe in Southwark in 1985: in both cases, he sees ideological projects dedicated to manufacturing a spurious national community, which in fact excludes the vast majority of the population. A more powerful continuity, however, persists in the fate of Cade: written in the years of Margaret Thatcher's violent suppression of the miners' strikes of 1984–5, Wilson's defence of Cade reads as a displaced defence of Arthur Scargill taking on Thatcher. Shakespeare's Cade of the 1590s, like the *Daily Mail*'s Scargill of the 1980s, encouraged acts of violence against the state, and in both cases, they were ruthlessly demonized by the cultural institutions of the British ruling classes.[11]

Finally, how is Shakespeare's treatment of Jack Cade likely to be interpreted in a neo-colonial context like South Africa? In Grahamstown itself, Shakespeare has been kept alive through the efforts of the Rhodes University English Department, the 1820 Settlers National Monument Committee and, more recently, the journal *Shakespeare in Southern Africa*. Jack Cade's survival has been less successful, though there is a brief sequel to Merriman's discussion of *2 Henry VI* in André Brink's 1996 critical study, which has the unintentionally ironic title *Destabilising Shakespeare* (published in Grahamstown by the Shakespeare Society of Southern Africa). Like Merriman and Patterson, Brink thinks Shakespeare is a genius, and like Merriman, Brink turns his attention from the Eastern Cape, and looks for instruction to philosophers and critics in the Northern Hemisphere, with the likes of Derrida and Montrose succeeding Merriman's dependence on Schlegel and Arnold. Unlike Merriman, however, Brink is interested in *2 Henry VI* not because of Jack Cade, but because of Margaret. Where Merriman focused anxiously on the class conflict in *2 Henry VI*, Brink is concerned exclusively with the gender dynamics of the play, arguing that Margaret is 'a fascinating spokesperson for the female scheming for survival within the restrictions of monarchy' (Brink 1996: 16).

Rather than conclude with Brink's silence on Cade, I would like to suggest reading Jack Cade in South Africa in the 1990s as a Renaissance Steve Biko. South African history of the 1970s and 1980s demonstrated at least two things that prompt a sympathetic consideration of *any* rebel leader like Cade: one, the extraordinary power of the state and its multiple organs to represent its opponents as 'rude and merciless' (*2 Henry VI* IV. iv. 32), and two, the necessary place of violent struggle in challenging tyranny and pursuing liberty. It would of course be difficult to sustain this reading of Cade in detail, but I would nonetheless suggest that each new context of *2 Henry VI* – including contemporary South Africa – demands a reinterpretation of Shakespeare's world, which will expose the ideological affiliations of professional scholarship.

Notes

1   The essays in the recent collection on *Postcolonial Shakespeares* (Loomba and Orkin 1998) all explore the connections between Shakespeare and colonial histories.
2   There has been a dramatic expansion in recent years in scholarship directed to exploring African philosophy, and the place of Africa in European philosophy. See, for example, Appiah 1992; Mudimbe 1988; Serequeberhan 1991; and Oruka 1990.

3 For Nathaniel Merriman's biography, see Whibley 1982 and Colchester 1926. Neither of these sources makes mention of Merriman's Shakespeare lectures.

4 For more detail on the emerging public sphere in the Eastern Cape during the 1850s, see Bank 1995: 189–236.

5 That Merriman was much preoccupied with the Indian Mutiny at the time of his Shakespeare lecture is borne out in a report 'Relief for India' in the same issue of the *Anglo-African* which describes his lecture. Whereas several hundred turned up for the Shakespeare lecture, only thirty were present to discuss relief for India. The report notes that '[r]esolutions expressive of deep sympathy, and of the necessity of immediate contributions in aid of their sufferings were passed', and Merriman's intervention at the meeting is described at some length:

> Archdeacon Merriman very earnestly pressed the introduction of the word 'Fellow-*Christians*' in conjunction with, if not entirely in place of 'Fellow-*Subjects*', – adding that to him the importance of the act of sympathy to be expressed by this meeting consisted in it being one of fellow-feeling with those who were sharers of a common faith, which included Natives as well as European subjects.
>
> (1857: 4)

6 James Adamson's lecture in Cape Town on *Modern Literature*, for example, contains a seventeen-page postscript on the work of Friedrich Schlegel (Adamson 1844: 23–40). The journeys of German Romantic thought to England during this period have been extensively researched. On A. W. Schlegel's influence in England, see Helmholtz-Phelan 1971; Sauer 1981; Ashton 1980: 62–3; Bate 1986: 9–15. On the relation between German and English Romanticism more generally, see Pipkin 1985.

7 On the ambiguous legacy of early German Romanticism to Aesthetic Theory, see de Man 1984; Bullock 1987; and the special issue of *Studies in Romanticism* (1992) 31, 4 on Walter Benjamin. The latent conservatism implicit in Schlegel's struggle with classicism is identified in Lacoue-Labathe and Nancy's observation that 'Romantic criticism . . . conceives of itself as the construction of classical works to come' (1986: 112).

8 The case for the centrality of the French Revolution in the development of German thought is made most powerfully by Herbert Marcuse in *Reason and Revolution*:

> German idealism has been called the theory of the French Revolution. This does not imply that Kant, Fichte, Schelling, and Hegel furnished a theoretical interpretation of the French Revolution, but that they wrote their philosophy largely as a response to the challenge from France to reorganize the state and society on a rational basis . . . Despite their bitter criticism of the Terror, the German idealists unanimously welcomed the revolution, calling it the dawn of a new era, and they all linked their basic philosophical principles to the ideals that it advanced.
>
> (1977: 3)

For a useful discussion of the German Romantics' shift to the right in the 1790s, see W. Daniel Wilson 1989: 131–59.

9 In *Are the Missionaries Mischief-Workers?* (1876), for example, Merriman looks back
   on the 1850s, and attacks the more extreme forms of settler racism.
10 Patterson's reading of Cade has received support from a number of US
   scholars. See, for example, Cartelli 1994: 58–9 and Caldwell 1995: 68–70.
11 Wilson's understanding of violence against the state is close to that of Georg
   Lukács and Walter Benjamin. In the essay 'Legality and illegality', Lukács concludes that for the working class 'the problem of legality and illegality is purely
   tactical in nature. It must be able to slough off both the cretinism of legality and
   the romanticism of illegality' (1974: 270). In 'Critique of violence', Benjamin is
   similarly caustic about the right of the state to dictate the terms of 'legitimate'
   violence: 'But all mythical, lawmaking violence, which we may call executive, is
   pernicious. Pernicious, too, is the law-preserving, administrative violence that
   serves it' (1979: 154). For a critical reading of Benjamin's essay, see Jacques
   Derrida's 'Force of law' (1992: 3–67).

6

Reading Shakespeare with intensity: A commentary on some lines from Nietzsche's *Ecce Homo*

SCOTT WILSON

When I seek my ultimate formula for *Shakespeare*, I always find only this: he conceived of the type of Caesar. That sort of thing can only be guessed: one either is it, or one is not. The great poet dips *only* from his own reality – up to the point where afterwards he cannot endure his work any longer.

When I have looked into my *Zarathustra*, I walk up and down in my room for half an hour, unable to master an unbearable fit of sobbing.

I know no more heart-rending reading than Shakespeare: what must a man have suffered to have such a need of being a buffoon!

Is Hamlet *understood*? Not doubt, *certainty* is what drives one insane. – But one must be profound, an abyss, a philosopher to feel that way. – We are all *afraid* of truth.

And let me confess it: I feel instinctively sure and certain that Lord Bacon was the originator, the self-tormentor of this uncanniest kind of literature: what is the pitiable chatter of American flat- and muddle-heads to *me*? But the strength required for the vision of the most powerful reality is not only compatible with the most powerful strength for action, for monstrous action, for crime – it even presupposes it.

We are very far from knowing enough about Lord Bacon, the first realist in every sense of that word, to know everything he did, wanted, and experienced in himself.

(Nietzsche 1969: 246)

I

> When I seek my ultimate formula for *Shakespeare*, I always find only this: he conceived of the type of Caesar.

At first sight, Nietzsche's statements on Shakespeare appear to be contradictory. In different parts of his *œuvre*, Nietzsche affirms both conflicting parties in *Julius Caesar* as essential to Shakespeare: belief in Brutus is 'the best thing' he can say in honour of Shakespeare (Nietzsche 1974: 98), while 'the ultimate formula' for Shakespeare is the Caesar 'type' (Nietzsche 1969: 246). This view is contradictory, however, only if it is assumed that one 'side' must be taken in a political allegory that warns against the dangers of either monarchy or regicide and revolution. In fact, Nietzsche is indifferent to conservative and liberal or neo-Marxist accounts of the play.[1]

It is Nietzsche's determination to think beyond the modern discourse of political emancipation that has made him so significant to a new generation of postmodern or hypermodern theorists and philosophers. Writers like Gilles Deleuze, for example, offer quite another form of emancipation or 'affirmation' that leaves behind, or steps aside from, the great political and philosophical work that has gone into the project of modernity. Rejecting the 'labour of the negative', Deleuze argues in his book *Nietzsche and Philosophy* that Nietzsche substitutes 'the practical element of *difference*, the object of affirmation and enjoyment [*jouissance*]' (Deleuze 1983: 9). For Deleuze, Nietzsche's will to power is essentially a will to affirm difference, and difference is affirmed through '*jouissance*' or '*joie*'. Thus, Brutus's assassination of Caesar is precisely motivated not by a wish to maintain a Roman or liberal democracy, but by his will to affirm his 'independence of soul' (Nietzsche 1974: 98). Writing of Shakespeare's play in *The Gay Science*, Nietzsche emphasizes the aristocratic values of Brutus, the 'honour' and 'virtue' that drive him to maintain the 'freedom of great souls' and sacrifice even his 'greatest friend' if he threatens this independence. The affirmation of individual sovereignty, his 'lofty morality', will sacrifice the absolute good, 'the grandest of men, the ornament of the world, the genius without peer' rather than be subjected to another (98).

At the limit, this 'lofty morality' that acknowledges nothing other than 'independence of soul' is opposed to the 'good' in every modern sense, either moral, political or economic. For Nietzsche, Brutus sacrifices Caesar for no 'good' reason – not for the greater good of Roman democracy, not even for the 'good' of 'political freedom', though Shakespeare has Brutus use this form of discourse as a 'symbol'. Such 'lofty morality' is closer to evil than to good, and, indeed, Nietzsche hints at some 'dark hour' or 'bad angel' that is veiled by Shakespeare's alleged 'political sympathy' with

Brutus's rhetoric. For Georges Bataille, Nietzsche's 'lofty morality' is a 'moral summit' wherein is located an evil that provides the strength and profundity of crime, of a monstrous action by which one would exceed the restricted economy of good and bad (Bataille 1992: 17). In such a moment, action would correspond 'to an exuberance of forces [bringing] about a maximum of tragic intensity' that exceeds and determines the modalities of the good (17). Bataille cites the crucifixion of Christ, held by Christians to be the greatest sin ever committed, as 'an extremely equivocal expression of evil' (17), a heterogeneous moment, or symbol, of excess that determines a new moral order. Both the execution of Christ and the assassination of Caesar constitute paradoxical 'crimes' that are constantly reiterated as points of intensity that bind together religious or political orders. It is a process that Nietzsche seems to repeat when he announces the death of God, and claims to have moved his philosophy 'beyond good and evil', a movement that simultaneously involves, and presupposes, a total re-evaluation of values and a genealogy of morals.

For any historicist criticism concerned with reading Shakespeare, Nietzsche's importance lies, accordingly, in his genealogical method of historical inquiry, a method taken up in recent years by Michel Foucault (see Foucault 1977). In the *Genealogy of Morals* (1887) and other texts, Nietzsche discovers the historical contingency of all values and decisively undermines any universal basis they might claim – in God, man, truth, nature, being, the body or labour. Trained as a philologist, Nietzsche's historical analyses attend closely to language and denote significant changes in the meaning of certain key terms, disclosing the historicity of areas that 'we tend to feel [are] without history – in sentiments, love, conscience, instincts' and so on (Foucault 1977: 139). The force driving historical transformations in meaning, Nietzsche believes, is the 'will to power', a 'primordial impulse' and 'principle of disequilibrium' that both shapes, and is deployed in, language and discourse (Klossowski 1997: 103). For Nietzsche there are historical significations, values, morals and so on that can be critically measured and evaluated, but there is also a measureless force that is beyond evaluation, a force that is indifferent to morality yet provides the very possibility of meaning and morality. As Jean-Luc Nancy suggests, for Nietzsche, 'power is not evaluated, it is the power to evaluate' (Nancy 1997: 128). There is no history without the will to power: it is the very process of extension and duration, the principle of historical unfolding.

While history might unfold, however, it does not 'progress'. Indeed, Nietzsche frequently invokes celebrated historical figures as a means of contesting the scientific claims of progressive historicism, as a way of proclaiming that 'the *goal of humanity* cannot lie in its end but only *in its highest exemplars*' (Nietzsche 1983: 111). Yet such reach and exemplarity do not simply reside in the historical specifics of time and place, historical 'role', 'significance', fame or infamy. The criterion for the process of selection is Nietzsche's doctrine of the Eternal Return of the Same, the notion that existence returns and repeats itself endlessly (the real always returns to its place). Given its mindless repetition, 'the brilliance of its absurdity and the absolute non-sense of existence' (Klossowski 1997: 160), the Eternal Return is the meaningless condition of all meaning, goal and purpose. Given also the horror or ecstasy that such a notion of endless recurrence must necessarily produce (see Nietzsche 1974: 341), and dependent upon its 'willing', the Eternal Return becomes the (non)basis upon which the constant transvaluation of all values can take place. Consequently, the historical figures that Nietzsche invokes are not selected as examples of those who have lived, as it were, according to such a doctrine, but because, as images, 'types' or metaphors, 'masks of the will to power', they connote the value of an intensity in Nietzsche (see Deleuze 1994: 41).

II

> . . . Caesar. That sort of thing can only be guessed: one either is it, or one is not. The great poet dips *only* from his own reality – up to the point where afterwards he cannot endure his work any longer.
>
> When I have looked into my *Zarathustra*, I walk up and down in my room for half an hour, unable to master an unbearable fit of sobbing.

In *Ecce Homo* Nietzsche associates himself closely with Shakespeare, one of a number of notable proper names that Nietzsche cites in this and other texts – Dionysus, Christ, Antichrist, Julius Caesar, Zarathustra. But these figures are not meant to be taken as real or mythical characters with whom one could simply 'identify'. Rather, they are, in the words of Gilles Deleuze, 'designations of intensity' (Deleuze 1985: 146). For Deleuze, 'pure intensities are like mobile individuating factors unwilling to allow themselves to be contained within factitious limits of this or that individual, this or that Self' (Deleuze 1994: 41). Deleuze's notion of 'intensity' is very close to Pierre Klossowski's use of the same term in *Nietzsche and the Vicious Circle*. For Klossowski, an intensity is the term for the fluctuations, the falling and rising, of unconscious 'impulses' that flow towards and between 'the code of everyday signs', signifiers of difference (the intensity of the Other). An intensity

> overflows the fixity of signs and continues on, as it were, in their intervals: each interval (thus each silence) belongs (outside the linkage of signs) to the fluctuations of an impulsive intensity. Is this the

'unconscious'? In itself, this term is merely a designation of the code of everyday signs that is applied afterward.

(Klossowski 1997: 37)

In relation to a signifying chain that channels and directs the impulses, an intensity is an effect of 'difference' – or rather it *is* difference (Deleuze 1994: 228). For Nietzsche the intensity of an impulsive identification that is signified by the introduction of a proper name rises at the point of difference and unknowing. Though historically remote and unreachable, Nietzsche nevertheless apprehends a 'Shakespeare' that resonates with his own reality: 'that sort of thing can only be guessed: one either is it, or one is not'. The intensity of difference is 'inexplicable' (Deleuze 1994: 228), it 'can be neither taught nor learnt' (Klossowski 1997: xix), but is apprehended, as difference, by the 'unexchangeable' singularity of the individual, or its 'soul', that is its 'irreducible and uncreated' depth (Klossowski 1997: x). 'The great poet dips *only* from his own reality.' Like Shakespeare, the image of Caesar is a 'simulacrum', an actualization of this 'reality', an obsessional image of something incommunicable and non-representational in Nietzsche. Moving from one simulacrum to another, the impulsive intensity moves down the chain of 'everyday signs', or, as Deleuze suggests, fluctuates in a 'perpetual displacement in the intensities designated by [other] proper names' metonymically linked with it (1985: 146).

In this passage from *Ecce Homo*, Nietzsche's impulsive intensity moves from Shakespeare to Caesar to Zarathustra to Shakespeare-as-buffoon to Hamlet to Lord Bacon. At each point these proper names function as metaphors or, to use Klossowski's vocabulary, 'simulacra': the imitative 'actualization of something in itself incommunicable and nonrepresentable' (1997: xi). As metaphors they betray the traces of an impulsive intensity, the fluctuations or vacillations of the will to power. As simulacra they are representations of something incommunicable and something that does not exist: 'Caesar' does not exist; all that exists is the incommunicable intensity that is bound to, and betrayed by, the simulacrum. A fundamental relationship is, then, established between a proper name, a simulacrum or metaphor, and an intensity that is manifested in an experience of pain: 'an unbearable fit of sobbing'. It is a relationship that has a long history, one that is sketched by Nietzsche in the second essay of *The Genealogy of Morals*.

Nietzsche argues, in the beginning of the second essay in *The Genealogy of Morals*, that intense pain is fundamental to the constitution of the human race and the binding together of its societies. There would be no human animal, there would be no memory, no knowledge, no history of any humanity without the primordial experience of pain and its continual infliction. Human history, self-consciousness, memory, self-awareness, do not derive from a social contract or some 'struggle for recognition', but from intensity or *jouissance*: the infliction and experience of unbearable agony. 'How can one create a memory for the human animal?' writes Nietzsche, 'how can one impress something upon this partly obtuse, partly flighty mind, attuned only to the passing moment, in such a way that it will stay there?' (1969: 60–1). Nietzsche's answer is simple: it must be burned in. Nietzsche delineates a strangely Promethean beginning to human history, but the theft of fire from the Gods is used not to cook food or warm the body: it is used to heat a branding iron so that, white hot, it can sear and mark human flesh, turning it into a property bearing the name of the master. Human law inscribes itself by burning itself into the flesh of an animal made human through the memory of its pain and the signifier, the proper name, that remains on the body as a mnemonic. If primordial 'man' became humanized by the use of a 'tool', it was not simply the utility of the object, its use in production, cultivation and so on that determined its importance in the destiny of humanity but its non-productive use as a weapon or instrument of torture, inscribing the knowledge of its making and its law on the human body as the memory of the human race. As Nietzsche notes, this act of marking, branding, signifying quickly became incorporated in religious practices that ritualized the entry of the subject into the human community as a form of sacrifice or castration, sometimes symbolically, but often literally: the sacrifice of goods, children, general mutilations, circumcisions, castrations and so on: human history begins with subjection to the signifier as a technology of castration, a tool saturated in blood and intensity.

For there to be human society, civilization, history, there must be a collective memory, collective pain held in an archive. Yet such a generalized 'marking' necessarily implies a power *of* the mark, a primordial impulse or will to power that punishes and drives the will to remember: it therefore implies an exception to the rule of the law. Behind the signifier, the tool or branding iron, is the trace of the primordial master – he who punishes but is not himself punished, someone who is the embodiment of the power to evaluate, measure, judge and punish, someone who is himself beyond measure, evaluation or judgement. Yet, never having been 'marked' or punished, the master can have no memory, no knowledge of his mastery; having no recall, no representation, no language to record himself and his history, he can *only* exist in the slavish representations of the punished. Consequently, the Nietzschean master is a mythical beast, a pre-historical creature that marks the transition from animal nature to human culture. As such the master is inseparable from the slavish fantasy that would imagine an originary, uncastrated, immensely powerful being: phallic, Godlike, without lack or fissure, identical to itself in its pure affirmation of itself, yet 'not much better than uncaged beasts of prey' (Nietzsche 1969: 40). *Uncaged* beasts of prey? This formulation of the primordial impulse presupposes a prior slavery, or an incarceration to a slavish principle that is the condition of the fantasy of absolute sovereignty. Nietzsche's nuance here is crucial because an intensity is not simply an effect of the painful binding to a signifier, or what psycho-analysis calls 'symbolic castration'. An intensity is also an effect of the ecstatic *unbinding* of an impulse from a signifier, the manifestation of a violent resistance to a master, the exuberance of an uncontrollable expenditure.

Nietzsche's designation of Shakespeare as a 'zone of intensity' is complex, and characteristic of his general attitude to the English dramatist throughout his work. That the invocation of Shakespeare should result in Nietzsche being 'unable to master an unbearable fit of sobbing' is not just because Shakespeare's name is seared into Nietzsche as that of a 'master'. Nor is it simply the acknowledgement that the authors of *Julius Caesar* and *Zarathustra* are not 'masters' at all but merely 'slaves' of representation (see Nietzsche 1969: 36 on the origin of representation in *ressentiment*). Rather, the sobbing exultation or abjection signifies a threshold of intensity that marks the limit of Nietzsche and himself, or at least his work. It is not clear to what extreme state 'the unbearable fit of sobbing' refers, but it seems, as the process of impulsive displacement continues, that in *Zarathustra* Nietzsche has met not the ultimate formula for Shakespeare but its nadir in his 'buffoonery'. Outside of *ressentiment* and the labour of the negative, 'buffoonery' has historically been the slave's only response to greatness. Significantly, then, it is not Shakespeare's greatness that provides the point of connection with Nietzsche, but the buffoonery that is imputed by him to suffering on the basis of his own; Nietzsche's pain, and the pain he perceives in Shakespeare, provides the thread and threshold to the past, to history, 'the code of everyday signs' and its channels of intensity.

III

> I know no more heart-rending reading than Shakespeare: what must a man have suffered to have such a need of being a buffoon!

At one level, the imputation of Shakespeare's 'buffoonery' is an aesthetic judgement that seems to be informed by the standard neo-classical reservation about 'indecorum' that is assumed by Nietzsche when he writes, in *Beyond Good and Evil*, of Shakespeare as 'that astonishing Spanish-Moorish-Saxon synthesis of tastes over which an ancient Athenian of the circle of Aeschylus would have half-killed himself with laughter or annoyance' (Nietzsche 1984: 134). These neo-classical reservations focus particularly on Shakespeare's mixing of genres, his unrelieving fondness for 'comic relief', and his indiscriminate bawdy punning that became, for Samuel Johnson, 'the fatal Cleopatra for which he lost the world, and was content to lose it' (Johnson 1969: 68).

But beyond aesthetic niceties, Nietzsche's view is also an acknowledgement that Shakespeare's *œuvre* is not the writing of a 'master', but a 'slave', a bourgeois – or at best a 'licenced fool' (even as the 'mask' of Lord Bacon). Shakespeare was writing at a time when the name and law of the master were being placed in question by the social, economic and religious upheavals introduced by the Reformation. The code of honour of the aristocratic, warrior caste was being subjected to a dual process of 'gentrification' and incredulity. In Elizabethan and Jacobean drama, for example, 'honour' comes under profound critical scrutiny. Occasionally it is invoked nostalgically, but more often than not it is presented satirically (Hotspur), cynically (Prince Hal) or subject to open ridicule (Falstaff), to cite just one play. The plays of Shakespeare and his contemporaries are part of a popular theatre that catered for the urban 'middling sort' of apprentices, tradesmen and artisans as well as the lower gentry, bureaucrats, politicians and financiers who would be so influential in the coming parliamentary struggle against the absolutist designs of the Stuart monarchy. Such a theatre, for Nietzsche, is clear evidence that 'the *plebeianism* of the modern spirit is of English origin' (Nietzsche 1969: 28). While Nietzsche affirms that it is possible to appreciate the 'artistic refinement' of the Elizabethan and Jacobean theatre, this can only occur despite 'the repellent fumes and the proximity of the English rabble in which Shakespeare's art and taste live' (Nietzsche 1984: 224). There is of course a heavily metaphorical air about these repellent fumes. They are also redolent of Puritan 'slave morality' and the kind of radical Protestantism that will provide, according to Nietzsche's contemporary Max Weber, 'the spirit of capitalism'. But Nietzsche could also have made a reasonable conjecture about the personal hygiene of Shakespeare's audience through the representations of crowds in his plays. In *Julius Caesar*, for example, Casca comments on the crowd's response as Caesar tests their enthusiasm for his ambitions:

> the rabblement hooted, and clapp'd their chopt hands, and threw up their sweaty night-caps, and uttered such a deal of stinking breath because Caesar refus'd the crown, that it had, almost, choked Caesar; for he swounded, and fell down at it. And for mine own part, I durst not laugh, for fear of opening my lips and receiving the bad air.
>
> (I. ii. 240–7)

It is probable that Nietzsche, for whom Shakespeare's Romans were 'nothing but flesh and blood Englishmen' (Nietzsche 1983: 85), believed this to be a fair account of an English audience. Casca's complaint is also interesting because it shows, at this stage of the play, popular support for the Republic. The crowd, famously, miss the plot and cheer Caesar *refusing* the laurel that is offered to him three times by his lieutenant Mark Antony when they are supposed to urge him to take it. The account also discloses, yet again in the play, the infamous physical weakness of Caesar, the 'feeble temper' that gives rise to him being called 'a sick girl' (I. ii. 127–8), and the need, felt by the Patricians, to *represent* themselves to the Plebeians, a need that implies that the ascendancy of the slaves' morality of representation is already presupposed. This does not necessarily change the basic structure of one class's domination over another, but it does change the mode of justification of that domination. Justifying mastery in terms of the slave's morality and desire might seem to make the master's rule ideologically strong, but it bases it in an inherent contradiction: it is difficult to govern *for* the people (as the Patricians claimed to do for the Plebeians) without heralding, as an inevitable consequence, government *by* the people.

In Elizabethan and Jacobean England there was no Republic, of course, nor any apparent prospect of one, but the absolutist project of the Tudors and the Stuarts disclosed a similar contradiction, and an inevitable collapse of aristocratic values. Not only did the unification of church and state require the monarchy formally to adopt priestly values (and in England's case, ultimately, Protestant and Puritan values), they also set out to 'persuade', through the so-called 'power of display', the urban population of their regal splendour and right to govern. The pomp and circumstance of royal or national tradition is continually being rewritten and reinvented every time a particular governing class recognizes itself, implicitly or otherwise, as lacking in some essential quality, some authentic nobility which it locates in 'tradition'. This moment occurs most powerfully for the first time in English history when the monarchy begins to come into its own as a genuine centralizing force. If the Tudors were the first English monarchs to give shape, form and substance to the splendour associated with regality, this was no doubt because they had a dubious right to a Crown they had taken by force. A large part of the Tudor Court consisted of *nouveaux riches* promoted by the Tudors at the expense of older aristocratic families who always claimed social superiority over the monarchy, as the Earl of Essex did, famously, over Elizabeth I. This sense of lack is perceptible paradoxically in the massive and ruinously expensive building projects undertaken in the sixteenth century by prominent members of the ever expanding Tudor Court (see Girouard 1980 and Wilson, S. 1992). The production of 'splendour' – of Versailles, and the Baroque Court of the Stuarts – signifies nothing so much as royal insecurity.

Correspondingly, it is precisely in response to such splendid excesses, designed to appeal to the gaze of the bourgeoisie, that the new aristocrats are condemned as decadent by Puritan writers. As soon as justification is sought, one way or another, in slave morality, the aristocracy immediately functions as its point of excess, its defining limit. For Nietzsche, the aristocracy becomes purely a 'function' of an alien morality, a 'corruption' of which aristocratic libertinage is merely a symptom (see Nietzsche 1984: 258). In the eyes of morality, hard work and self-reliance, splendour and luxury become licentiousness and sleaze. The *jouissance* of the 'master' is conceived as evil, as the non-productive, useless expenditure of the fruits of the 'slave's' labour: *ressentiment* is primed and ready to take on revolutionary force. Consistent with the 'reactive' nature of this force, however, 'the people' do not revolt with a good conscience. According to British folklore, when the executioner's axe descended on the neck of Charles I a loud groan of anguish and ecstasy rose from the crowd (Wilson, R. 1992: 18). However coldly rational the Puritan regicides determined to be, Charles's execution has been popularly recalled as an extraordinary moment of transgression producing an involuntary expression of collective *jouissance* in the sense of a form of ecstasy bound up with horror and anguish rather than simple revenge or pleasure. The law of rational government, to which everyone would now be subject, was engendered and embodied in a new experience of criminal excess, horror and terror, that would remain its defining form. The monarchy had its link to divinity irrevocably severed, but this merely opened up – in anguish and excitement – the apprehension of secular evil. It was as if the Enlightenment axe flashed for an instant, and, like a lightning bolt giving a black intensity to the night it denies, illuminated the darkness of modernity's transgressive future after 1649.

Much of this history was pre-empted and imaginatively prepared by *Julius Caesar* and the theatrical construction of the 'Caesar-type'. Ancient Rome and Julius Caesar were points of negotiation and contestation between Puritan forces and monarchical forces. *Julius Caesar*, it might be argued, sees the supersession of an ancient model of political sovereignty, in which the role of the master is taken over by the signifier as 'the last philosophical metamorphosis of the despot' (Deleuze 1985: 149). Like the Cromwellian Commonwealth, the law of the new Roman Empire was based in crime, in bloody murder and violent insurrection. While 'the People' becomes the master signifier for the Commonwealth or Republic, the New Roman Empire locates its authority in a name – 'Caesar' – rather than an individual, or rather, in an individual insofar as he operates in its name.

'What should be in that "Caesar"?' asks Cassius ingenuously of Brutus, 'Why should that name be sounded more than yours? / Write them together, yours is as fair a name' (I. ii. 140–2). But kings, dictators and emperors down the ages have found more to approve in the sound of 'Caesar' than in 'Brutus'. The ironic thing about Julius Caesar is of course that he never becomes 'Caesar'. Assassinated before he can make himself emperor, it is only his *name* that goes on to wear the monarchical laurel with Augustus. It is curious that so many monarchs, emperors, absolutist czars, shahs, Kaisers and so on should seek to authorize and legitimate their – in most cases – divine right to rule on a man who *wasn't even king*. Julius Caesar was only a Roman general. And yet, after his death, his name was swiftly to become synonymous with absolute authority – all the subsequent Roman emperors named themselves after him.

Why should the name of a Roman general who *fails* in his attempt to become king take on such primordial status? There are any number of stories about regicides, murdered kings and emperors, the 'Sad tales of the death of kings', as Richard II laments. Legend and history are filled with such tales both before and after the death of Julius Caesar, before and after Shakespeare's play. One reason might be that 'Caesar', as the term for the would-be emperor who failed to live up to the promise of his own name, performs the double operation required by the Tudor doctrine of the King's Two Bodies. This doctrine acknowledges the necessity that the monarchy be split between a spiritual body signifying the divinity of the state and a natural body in which that spirit is incarnated, but which is also subject to decay and death. While a particular monarch is never identical to either body, his or her fate is ultimately tied to the body natural. The doctrine accounts for the fact that even though individual monarchs die, the office is immortal. At the same time, since the doctrine separates individual from state, it therefore legitimates the removal of an individual, if not the system, if the body natural is perceived to be particularly subject to moral and physical decay, or degeneration. *Jouissance* is split, then, between the eternally castrating power of the paternal metaphor and the disgusting *jouissance* of the body that may, in its name, be cut off. A signifier, being nothing, does not enjoy in itself; others enjoy, in various ways, in its name, even *for* it. Since the master signifier evacuates all intensity, all enjoyment and pain from the symbolic centre of the law, it becomes reassociated with its fantasy body, with the enjoyment of the 'body natural', and with its spectacular fall. The Roman emperors who followed the death of Julius Caesar – Augustus, Tiberius, Caligula, Claudius, Nero – all called themselves Caesar and all enjoyed reigns that would become notoriously associated with excess, degeneration and decadence, an excess that would also, to a significant degree, come to define monarchy in the early modern period, eventually justifying both its overthrow and its continued existence as the spectacle for bourgeois moral desire.

The importance of *Julius Caesar*, as a play that dramatizes the emergence of the paternal metaphor in its modern form, lies in the struggle between its charismatic and rationalist justifications characterized by Mark Antony and Brutus. The former deploys the hideous spectacle of Caesar's 'natural' or 'real' body, in the form of his bleeding corpse, to dazzle the assembled crowd and rouse its affections to mutiny; the latter appeals, ineffectually, in the name of the 'symbolic' body politic of the Republic, to reason. History, however, is with Brutus. The history of the English, French and Russian revolutions (among others) has shown that the more the paternal metaphor is grounded in reason, the more hideous becomes the body of the ruling classes that luxuriate and enjoy in the name of paternal authority.

That Julius Caesar and the legends surrounding his death, the succession of 'Caesars' that followed him and his links with northern Europe, were important reference points in the struggle over the political future of the monarchy in the seventeenth century was a fact widely exploited in the commercial theatre. It was an exploitation acknowledged by Shakespeare in a variety of ironies that are deliberately embedded in his play, the most notable being Cassius's exclamation in the bloody wake of the assassination: 'How many ages hence / Shall this our lofty scene be acted over, / In states unborn and accents yet unknown!' (III. i. 111–13). Shakespeare's little self-reflexive joke in the midst of tragedy is characteristic of the buffoonery lamented by Nietzsche, but also recognized in himself. As Shakespeare's company replay the assassination scene once more, and the replayed end and origin of another unborn state is declared in another unknown accent, the comedy of eternal recurrence is revealed again in the laughter that announces its absolute non-sense. If that were not enough, Shakespeare repeats the scene almost immediately in *Hamlet* (first performed in 1600–2, shortly after *Julius Caesar*) as a means of lightening or tightening, with another bit of buffoonery, the tension of Hamlet's entrapment in the vicious circle of the two regicides. Hamlet jests and puns with Polonius, the actor-politician, who boasts that he 'did enact Julius Caesar. I was killed i'th' Capitol. Brutus killed me', even as the actor-playing-Hamlet, in the presence of the king, acknowledges in anticipation that 'It was a brute part of him to kill so capital a calf there' (*Hamlet* III. ii. 102–5).[2]

IV

> Is Hamlet *understood*? Not doubt, *certainty* is what drives one insane. – But one must be profound, an abyss, a philosopher to feel that way. – We are all *afraid* of truth.

The problem of Shakespeare's buffoonery, following the path of Nietzsche's impulsive intensity, inevitably leads to Hamlet whose own antic disposition and famous disarticulation from his role and destiny have been endlessly reassessed. Pierre Klossowski's reading of this passage from *Ecce Homo* (Klossowski 1997: 204–7) comes at the culmination of two chapters that look closely, if sometimes elliptically, at Nietzsche's intensive identification with Hamlet – or at least with the German Romantic and Freudian Hamlet. In chapters on 'The consultation of the paternal shadow' and 'The most beautiful invention of the sick', Klossowski discusses Nietzsche's variation on the Oedipal schema that is apparently introduced, in the form of a riddle, in the first chapter of *Ecce Homo*: 'I am', writes Nietzsche, 'already dead as my father, but as my mother I am still alive and growing old' (Klossowski 1997: 172; Nietzsche 1969: 222). Reading *Ecce Homo* in conjunction with some of Nietzsche's juvenile reminiscences (as a child growing up in the shadow of his mother's bereavement and mourning for his dead father) and accounts of dream work, Klossowski assesses Nietzsche's negative identification of his father as a 'decadent'. This is a judgement consistent with his view of the degeneration of the paternal figure generally (the death of God), and Klossowski connects it with what he believes was Nietzsche's desire to occupy the symbolic place of the mother in order to 'give birth to himself anew and [become] his own creature' (Klossowski 1997: 178), a desire also manifested in his actual hostility to his real mother and sister. The death of the father, who was for Nietzsche never anything other than a symbol, released a 'spectre of *madness* and the *abyss*, into which the gaze of the self-constructing youth fell, fascinated' (178). But 'when you gaze long into an abyss, the abyss also gazes into you' (Nietzsche 1984: 146). And it was to Nietzsche's gaze, staring into the madness of the abyss disclosed by the death of the father, that were revealed the principles of the Eternal Return, principles that replaced the law of the father with a 'maternal' principle of becoming. Klossowski outlines an analysis that sketches out a 'complex' delineated in mythic form in which the paternal figure is reduced to the monstrous, primordial impulse of the Minotaur, and the maternal or filial bond provides the thread of becoming in the labyrinth of the Eternal Return of the Same (Klossowski 1997: 197): a labyrinth formulated in 'language' (or a general textuality) in which the difference that marks repetition is announced:

> I am confined *somewhere* and I will never manage to *find* myself again: the message the prisoner sends to me is unintelligible; I am shut up inside language, and what belongs to me lies on the *outside*, in the time which the universe follows and which history recounts: the *memory* that outlives humans is *my mother*, and the *Chaos* that turns around on itself is my *father*.
>
> (1997: 185)

In Pierre Klossowski's reading of Nietzsche's identification with Hamlet and Shakespeare in this passage from *Ecce Homo*, 'certainty' is located at the point of intensity, in the labyrinth, where identification meets its limit in the apprehension of difference: 'It is the certainty of the irreducible depth whose muteness has no equivalent' (Klossowski 1997: 204). This certainty 'drives one insane', however, when the 'abyss' gazes back as a reflection of the monstrosity, the Minotaur, that lies at the irreducible depth of the soul. Yet these reflections, the monstrous simulacra of myth and the imagination (of which the Minotaur is a prime example) do not do justice to the power that would bring them into being. The certainty that drives one insane is, for the philosopher Nietzsche, as it is for Hamlet, and as he imagines it is for Shakespeare, that the power of the primordial impulse does not simply lie in the monstrous or criminal act, but is prior to the power of conceiving, imagining or representing that would make the monstrous or criminal act possible. Even knowledge itself is '*an unacknowledged power of monstrosity*' (Klossowski 1997: 205). All action, even ethical action, takes its bearings from the impulse that springs from the abyss of non-meaning, from the 'blind spot' that is the condition of all reflection, thought and negativity.[3]

V

And let me confess it: I feel instinctively sure and certain that Lord Bacon was the originator, the self-tormentor of this uncanniest kind of literature: what is the pitiable chatter of American flat- and muddle-heads to *me*? But the strength required for the vision of the most powerful reality is not only compatible with the most powerful strength for action, for monstrous action, for crime – it even presupposes it.

We are very far from knowing enough about Lord Bacon, the first realist in every sense of that word, to know everything he did, wanted, and experienced in himself.

Nietzsche finds in Shakespeare, then, the 'uncanniest kind of literature' since it constructs its author as a 'mask' in order to hint at the 'monstrous' dispositions that are thereby concealed in the work. This is why, as an effect of his identification, Nietzsche supposes 'Lord Bacon' – the statesman, lawyer, philosopher, empiricist and tormentor of nature and Catholic recusants – to have been the true author of the drama. Consequently, Klossowski characterizes *Ecce Homo* in a similar way as an uncanny form of double writing in which a pseudonymous Nietzsche (the buffoon) writes absurd propaganda for the concealed, monstrous authority 'who will decide both the future and the moral and spiritual orientation of his generation' (Klossowski 1997: 207). What confirms Lord Bacon as the true identity of

'Shakespeare' is not the historical evidence put forward by the 'pitiable chatter' of the American Baconians, nor is it just the sympathy that Nietzsche might feel for a fellow philosopher, rather it is the notoriety of Bacon, the intimations of corruption and evil that darken his reputation, the 'crime' that is 'presupposed' by 'the vision of the most powerful reality'. Most notably, Bacon was convicted, in 1621, for accepting bribes as Lord Chancellor (Nietzsche 1969: 246).[4]

Remarkably, then, it is not the gaze of Old Hamlet (famously played by Shakespeare) that lies at the source of Nietzsche's paternal identification, the 'spectre' of the 'paternal shadow'. It is the gaze of the regicide Claudius. Lord Bacon, in the aspect that Nietzsche would recall him, is much closer to the corrupt and fratricidal killer of Hamlet's father, and the lover of his mother. Indeed, this makes good (Freudian) sense to one who would identify with the son who attributed so much significance to the desire of the mother. For Freud, the source of Hamlet's 'neurosis' – his procrastination and his supposed madness – lies in this unconscious identification with, and desire for, the source of Claudius's potency in the *jouissance* of the mother (see Lacan 1977b). Herein lies the equivocality of Nietzsche when, in the shadow of a dead father, he seeks an identification with a symbolic mother who will have been infused with the potency of the primordial impulse in order to give birth to a 'new Nietzsche'. It is precisely the sort of reasoning that drives Hamlet, in his feigned or fervid madness, to call Claudius his 'mother' (IV. iii. 52–5).

With this foreclosure from the law of the father and the gaze of Old Hamlet, this hypostatizing of the mother as, at once, the bearer of primordial *jouissance* and the nurturing matrix of the efficient 'functioning of his corporeal machine (the promotion of the body to the rank of a higher intelligence)' (Klossowski 1997: 186), Nietzsche opens out the possibility of a desire that is at once 'feminized' and 'impersonal' (Land 1992: 26). By removing the 'bunk hole of masculinity', such a desire sets in play an unrestricted 'Dionysian economy [that is] the flux of impersonal desire', flowing in 'resurgent waves of intensity' (Land 1992: 26). In setting the co-ordinates of such a desire, Nietzsche laid out, for some, the deoedipalized, psychological structure of 'desiring capital' into the twenty-first century. For one 'anti-oedipal' late twentieth-century strand of post-Nietzschean 'schizoanalysis', there is no law but the pure functionality of the impulses (machinic desire) and the maternal enjoinment to desire in the cause of a general productivity: a total 'universe of productive and reproductive desiring-machines, universal primary production' (Deleuze and Guattari 1972: 5; see also Land 1993).

In an analogous development, the cultural history of the Anglo-American West has also been governed, across a range of its ideological

representations, by one particular 'intensity': its idolatry of a certain reading of a Hamlet who provides the hinge, the double-bind, of oedipalization
and deoedipalization. Here is a 'rebellious' Hollywood Hamlet transfixed
by the reflection of his own impotence in the death and 'castration' of his
father; a Hamlet who rages at the spectre of evil that the death of the father
introduces, yet revels in the endless production of violent images that his
spectre seems to justify; a Hamlet who constantly *acts out* the fantasy of
maternal enjoyment, constantly simulates and stimulates the *jouissance* of the
mother in the name of a generalized hyperproductivity. One agent of the
constant stimulation of the reproductive body is, of course, the cult of
eternal youth and youthful rebellion, the hysterical rejection of paternal law
for the approval of the phantasmatic mother who embodies a kind of *jouissance* that attracts and repels at once. This fantasmatic, symbolic mother sets
the parameters of the good (both ideological and economic) in terms of
functionalist libertarianism (the billion-dollar porn industry, for example)
and the hygienic, airbrushed efficiency of latter-day apple pie puritanism.
Here is the indifferent repetition of absolute commodification in which the
impulses and affects of an impersonal desire 'revolve around objects with no
value' (Nietzsche cited in Klossowski 1997: 208).

The 'type of Caesar' that Nietzsche considered 'the ultimate formula for
Shakespeare' is, then, not an individual or a character or a simulacrum or
even a signifier. The 'type' is a 'phantasm', in the same way that the Eternal
Return is a phantasm (Klossowski 1997: xi). For Klossowski, a phantasm is
'an obsessional image' produced by the impulses. In *Julius Caesar* Julius
Caesar barely exists as a character or image at all. He makes some brief
appearances in the first two acts, but is dead before the play is half over. But
this is the whole point of Caesar: he is assassinated. The phantasm of the
'Caesar-type' precisely concerns the image of Caesar's assassination; it is in
his assassination that the lives of the impulses find their expression. That is
why 'the best thing' Nietzsche can say of Shakespeare is that 'he believed in
Brutus'.

As a self-creating force of pure affirmation, the will to power, or primordial impulse, is not accessible to any man or woman endowed with self-
consciousness, thought or language, since any form of reflection that might
access it involves the power of an action, drawn from the same source, that
negates it. The creature of the primordial impulse is simply a God, a
machine (a God machine) or a beast of prey. The primordial impulse is not
embodied in the military exploits of Caesar, the Roman General, but its
presence is discernible over the horizon when Caesar crosses the Rubicon in
search of immortality, when Brutus learns that 'this man / Is now become a
god' (I. ii. 114–15). The primordial impulse comes into being only in the

form of 'a maximum of tragic intensity' at the moment of Caesar's slaughter. 'To kill God to return him to this nothingness he is and to manifest his existence at the centre of a light that blazes like a presence – for the ecstasy' (Foucault 1998: 26). For Nietzsche, the assassination of Caesar is *both* an effect of the threat Brutus perceives to 'the independence' of his soul, and the purest expression of that independence. In Klossowski's terms, the imperceptible, 'unexchangeable depth of the soul' finds its outward intensity (the recognition of its difference) in that moment of pure expenditure. If there is an ethical dimension to the phantasm it would be because, like the 'Thing' that articulates ethics and desire in psychoanalysis (Lacan 1992: 80), the phantasm articulates the impulses at a point of intensity, at the point of the non-exchangeable singularity of the 'soul', that resists all modes of 'extensity' that would explicate, regulate and homogenize it (Deleuze 1994: 230). If the death of God continues to give shape to contemporary experience (Foucault 1998: 26), it is only insofar as it provides the 'explosive reality' for an intensity that resists all forms of slavish existence.

It is in relation to the phantasm of this Caesar-type, then, that the 'perpetual displacement' of Nietzsche's 'nomad thought' circulates around the 'abyss' or the 'chaos' disclosed by the death of God and the revelation of the Eternal Return. The phantasm provides the point of connection and disconnection with the Other in the form of the proper name, the signifier. In this passage from *Ecce Homo*, the intensity of the phantasm is encountered in unbearable experiences that propel Nietzsche beyond himself to the point of an unknowing connection marked and veiled by Shakespeare's bawdy 'buffoonery', his weakness for the 'fatal Cleopatra', by the pain and recognition of suffering, by the certainty (and necessity) of an evil that provides the strength and profundity of crime, of a monstrous action by which one would exceed the restricted moral economy of good and bad.

The generalization of the restricted economy is always equivocal, however. An economy can always be 'generalized' for useful, that is moral or hypermoral, purposes. As Hamlet himself suggests, this is another meaning of the Caesar-type, the Alexander-type or even the Brutus-Hamlet-type, that is given up to the revolutions of the Eternal Return, the return that turns the Caesar-type to dust:

Hamlet: Alexander died, Alexander was buried, Alexander returneth
         to dust, the dust is earth, of earth we make loam, and
         why of that loam whereto he was converted might
         they not stop a beer-barrell?
         Imperious Caesar, dead and turn'd to clay,
         Might stop a hole to keep the wind away.
         O, that that earth, which kept the world in awe

Should patch a wall t'expel the winter's flaw.
But soft, but soft awhile. Here comes the King.

(Hamlet V. i. 201–10)

Caesar is here returned to the eternal transmutation of matter in a general economic, vicious circle of exchanges, debts and returns. Hamlet describes a general economy in which great generals, divine emperors and sovereigns are put to use in the most abject and slavish manner. Caesar is returned to dust, repaying his debt to the bloody piece of earth that, in death, gave him birth, exchanging the laurel of imperial might for the bite of the winter's wind. Perhaps this is a Christian homily on the hubris of human vanity; or perhaps this is the melancholic testament to the tragedy of the Caesar-type, a tragedy encompassing the pit and pinnacle of sacred and profane desires upon which republican and monarchic orders have been staked. Or perhaps this is an uncanny premonitory vision of some kind of material future in which a 'Caesar' still has a place, but the place of a heroic, ceremonial or constitutional bung hole: a future in which an absolutely totalizing and homogenizing economy instrumentalizes the ultimate in sovereign human aspirations to pure utility.

Nietzsche pre-empted the 'general economy' of Bataille when he defined evil as excess in relation to the hygienic, moral rationalizations of a bourgeois restricted economy. 'Just as *"evil"* can be considered exaggeration, disharmony, disproportion, *"the good"* may be a *protective diet* against the danger of exaggeration, disharmony, disproportion' (Nietzsche cited in Klossowski 1997: 82). But, as Klossowski notes, 'if excess is merely an exaggerated state, a magnification of a normal state, then what is a normal state?' (84). And what if the 'normal state' is one of inordinate excess such as that which characterizes hypermodernity (see Goux 1998)? This 'normal state' is no longer regulated by a 'Caesar', a signifier that would function as a point of heterogeneity or intensity that regulates and evaluates the impulses. Instead, the dust of Caesar would fail even to provide an adequate cap to stop the 'endless precession of simulacra' pouring from the bottle of Budweiser of 'the evil demon of images'. The intoxication of these images that flow from the 'Caesar's Palace' thrill factory of North America induce a dulling of the senses, a falling off of intensity, and a waning of affect (see, for example, Jameson 1991). But that is the risk of the Eternal Return, the very wager of excess that brings it into being, the drunken impulse to make a difference:

> let us express what lies at the *depth* of all things in a monstrous form. For if we declare that this depth is unknowable, we will always cut the figure of an *easy-going agnosticism*, which will change nothing in the

behaviour of humanity, nor in its morality, nor in its forms of existence. But if we speak the language of the impostor-fool, everything will be completely different; and therefore we say this absurd thing: *everything returns!*

(Klossowski 1997: 221–2)

And it is precisely in the return from the 'depths' of that unknowable force that fails to circulate in the hypereconomic, vicious cycle of absolute utility that the difference will be made.

Notes

1 See Wilson, R. 1992 for a good account of traditional political readings.
2 G. R. Hibbard, the editor of the Oxford edition of the play, notes that these lines suggest that it is likely that the actors Richard Burbage and John Heminges would have played the corresponding roles Brutus/Hamlet and Julius Caesar/Polonius, respectively (Hibbard 1987: 3–4).
3 See Botting and Wilson 1997b for a complementary reading of *Hamlet* in the terms of Bataillean and Hegelian-Marxist negativity.
4 See also Nietzsche 1968: 848 for further identifications of Shakespeare and Bacon as a 'moral monster'.

Shakespeare's monster of nothing
HOWARD CAYGILL

Alonso: I heard nothing.
Antonio: O, 'twas a din to fright a monster's ear,
        To make an earthquake!
                    (*The Tempest* II. i. 308–10)

'To be or not to be' is not the only question Shakespeare asks before the spectre of nothing, nor do its terms - being and not-being – exhaust the possibilities of Shakespearean ontology. The role played by nothing in Shakespeare's dramas is far more equivocal than anything dreamt of in philosophy; in them Shakespeare 'monsters' the equivocal spectacle of nothing,[1] but without arriving at an affirmation of being. The performative negation of nothing issues in the equivocal condition of not-nothing, a state that is neither being nor nothing. This condition is exemplified by the treatment of the ancient ontological maxim *ex nihilo, nihil fit* – 'out of nothing comes nothing' – in *King Lear*. Out of Cordelia's 'nothing' and Lear's citation of the maxim 'nothing will come of nothing, Speak again' (I. i. 90) comes neither unequivocal being nor unequivocal not-being but a series of equivocal events linked by dissension, betrayal, civil war and madness – not being but not nothing.

  The equivocal philosophical drama of nothing and not-nothing is worked through in a number of Shakespeare's plays, but in ways which defy the rules of philosophical demonstration. For philosophers, *ex nihilo, nihil fit* marks the beginning of a philosophical drama in which the equivocal character of nothing is neutralized by the negation of nothing becoming the affirmation of being. The philosophical demonstration of the passage from being to nothing and back shuns the equivocal monster of nothing that presides over Shakespeare's plays. This appears repeatedly as the impossible state of a nothing that is something or the double-negative or 'not-nothing' that remains stalled in a melancholy state of 'heavy nothing', refusing to move from the negation of nothing to the affirmation of being. Indeed, Shakespeare's equivocal nothing and the puns, fallacies and conceits that accompany it appear sophistical and even repugnant to good philosophical taste.

The contrast between the nothing of the philosophers and that of Shakespeare is evident from the significance given to the transition from nothing to being in the ontologies of Hegel and Heidegger. The movement from nothing to being by means of becoming is the explicit object of discussion in Hegel's *Logic* (1812–16), and informs its entire demonstration. In order to initiate this movement Hegel found it necessary to confront *ex nihilo, nihil fit*, describing the maxim as 'one of those propositions to which great importance was ascribed in metaphysics' and from which two opposed conclusions could be drawn. The first was the pagan eternity of the world – the claim that the world did not emerge out of nothing, but that there was always something – while the other was the doctrine of divine creation: 'Later, especially Christian, metaphysics, whilst rejecting the proposition that nothing comes of nothing, asserted a transition from nothing into being' (Hegel 1969: 84). Both positions save the *ex nihilo, nihil fit*, but in ways which assume the priority of being – cosmic or divine – over nothing.

Hegel's formal demonstration of the emergence of being from nothing relies on double negation: nothing is understood as the negation of being which is itself negated in a return to being. The concept of 'nothing' as an abstract negation of being is itself negated by showing that it is a 'determinate negation' of a determinate being. For Hegel, nothing is never the accomplished negation of being in general but always a 'determinate' negation of a particular being. The equivocal characteristics of nothing – exploited by Shakespeare – are in this view fallacious, arising from a determinate negation which misrecognizes itself as total negation. Such misrecognition would seem to be exemplified by the negations of King Leontes in his fit of jealousy in I. ii. of *The Winter's Tale*: 'is this nothing? / Why then the world, and all that's in't, is nothing, / The covering sky is nothing, Bohemia nothing, / My wife is nothing, nor nothing have these nothings, / If this be nothing' (I. ii. 292–6). Under Hegelian auspices, nothing as the negation of the world, the sky, Bohemia and the king's wife is determinate while the nothing of these nothings is an abstraction, a misrecognition. The king intensifies the nothingness of the world, sky, Bohemia and his wife through the final negation – they cannot even be nothing; they are expelled even further into the void by being denied nothing. For Hegelian logic, Leontes's negation of the negation – the reduction to nothing of the reductions to nothing of the world, sky, Bohemia and the queen – rather than intensifying their nothingness would return them all to being. If nothing is itself nothing, then the world, the sky, Bohemia and the queen all return to existence.

In Hegel's demonstration the priority of Being over nothing is asserted according to pagan or Christian premises; it is not demonstrated, nor does he ever entertain the possibility of a movement between nothing and not nothing prior to that between being and nothing. For the same reason – the assumed priority of being – the idea central to Shakespeare that nothing can 'be' substantial or 'heavy' while not possessing being, is absent in Hegel. Since reality is inconceivable without the attribute of being, nothing is incapable of any reality apart from being, especially since it is but the illusory effect of a determinate negation. To conceive a reality that would not partake of being is monstrous within the terms of Hegelian ontology, since it places an indeterminate relation between nothing and not-nothing (a reality that is not necessarily being) prior to the determinate relation between being and nothing.

The abhorrence of the equivocations of nothing is even more marked in Heidegger's *Introduction to Metaphysics* (1935). The point of departure for Heidegger's inquiry into being and nothing is parochially ontological, beginning with the question 'Why are there beings rather than nothing?' The fundamental question already assumes its ontological answer, indeed goes further by 'cross[ing] out the superfluous words "rather than nothing" and limit[ing] the sentence to the simple and strict form: "Why are there beings?"' (Heidegger 1987: 23–4). Crossing out, however, leaves nothing there, prompting Heidegger to reflect that 'this speaking of nothing remains in general repellent to thought, and in particular demoralizing' (24). He proposes an authentic speaking of nothing, warning of the dangers of the 'cheap acid of a merely logical intelligence' (26), such as indeed he would find exemplified in Shakespeare's repellent and demoralizing monster of nothing.

Even after conceding that 'there is something very interesting about nothing' (27), Heidegger lets it slip away by focusing on why there are beings. Nothing serves as a supplement that allows him to ask the ontological question, allowing him to conceal the more general form of the question 'why is there not nothing rather than nothing?' by framing it in the derived form of '"why are there beings?"' (27). The question of being thus emerges from distinction of being and nothing, an outcome that is neither repellent nor demoralizing. This stagecraft is classically philosophical, departing from different premises but arriving at an outcome similar to Hegel: nothing is convertible into being. Nothing is univocally linked with being. This ignores ways of thinking the relation of nothing and not-nothing other than in terms of being and not-being, and it is here that Shakespeare's performative play with the equivocations of nothing and not-nothing can become instructive for philosophy.

Shakespeare's transformation of the philosophical commonplaces of being and nothing into the equivocal monster of nothing and not-nothing is staged in a number of ways. The first and most characteristic is to make nothing into a substantive by speaking of it as if it were real. The second is to play with the logical properties of double negation: nothing is the negation of being, but the negation of nothing does not automatically restore the original condition of being; in other words, for Shakespeare, the negation of the negation has no definite result. For the negation of nothing does not result in something, but leaves both thing and nothing suspended. The vertiginous properties of these two ways of monstering nothing are played out in the histories around the thing of nothing that is the monarch. The third staging of the equivocation of nothing denies *ex nihilo, nihil fit* by what philosophically would be regarded as the fallacious elision of discursive and figural orders.[2] Shakespeare systematically elides nothing, the recently discovered and for Elizabethan culture still equivocal mathematical concept of zero or 'cipher' and its icon 0 with the vocative 'O'. The pun may now seem mannered, but it was evidently recognized and enjoyed by Elizabethan audiences; indeed, it is precisely the equivocation between the iconic zero and the vocative 'O' that ignites the 'muse of fire' evoked in the prologue to *Henry V*.

A fairly pure example of the conversion of nothing into a thing without being occurs in *Richard III* in the king's resort to swearing by nothing. Nothing becomes the condition for his oath, but it is precisely this condition that makes his oath implausible. In an exchange between Richard and Queen Elizabeth, Richard seeks something credible by which he can swear: he tries his chivalry (his 'George' his 'Garter'), his crown, the world, his father's death, himself, God, the time to come – by anything and everything – only to be left with nothing:

K. Richard: I swear –
Elizabeth: By nothing, for this is no oath:
        Thy George, profan'd, hath lost his lordly honour;
        Thy Garter, blemish'd, pawn'd his knightly virtue;
        Thy crown, usurp'd, disgrac'd his kingly glory.
        If something thou wouldst swear to be believ'd,
        Swear then by something that thou hast not wrong'd.

(IV. iv. 368–73)

In a clear equivocation, the king must swear by something he has not wronged, which is nothing, for there is nothing he has not wronged, but to swear by nothing 'is no oath'. Nothing thus becomes not-nothing, but this does not make it a thing that can be affirmed in an oath. The oath upon nothing shows that it cannot possess the same reality as other beings: while it can be negated to become not-nothing it cannot be affirmed as a being.

Rather than convert nothing into being, Shakespeare opens an in-between state – not-nothing – which is neither being nor nothing. The negation of nothing is intrinsically equivocal, appearing at the same time as a nothing that is a thing, and a thing that is nothing. The classic example of this in-between state of not-nothing is the Shakespearean monarch, the definitive thing of nothing. The lessons of Shakespeare's histories of the monarchy are summed up by Hamlet during his interrogation by Rosencrantz and Guildenstern as to the whereabouts of the corpse of Polonius:

Rosencrantz: My lord, you must tell us where the body is and go with us to the King.
Hamlet: The body is with the King, but the King is not with the body. The King is a thing –
Guildenstern: A thing, my lord?
Hamlet: Of nothing. Bring me to him.

(IV. ii. 24–9)

The equivocation of Hamlet's conclusion that 'the King is a thing of nothing' operates on several levels. As Kantorowicz has shown in his classic *The King's Two Bodies* (1957), the institution of monarchy does not exist unequivocally: it is more than the thing or particular body of the reigning monarch. The reigning monarch is with, or embodies, atemporal kingship, but such kingship always exceeds the body of any particular monarch. The reigning monarch, who would embody kingship, can never fully do so, and is thus also an embodiment of nothingness. The king is a thing only in so far as he embodies kingship, but since he cannot ever fully do so, he is nothing.

This reading is consistent with the Platonic premises of Kantorowicz's argument, which make a division between the idea of the king and the actual king. But the complications of Shakespeare's understanding of the thing of nothing are even more intricate. A further equivocation follows from the particular pretensions of the new king, Hamlet's uncle. Hamlet consistently refuses his claim to be king, insisting that the real king is his dead father. The king is dead, a corpse or a thing of nothing. The dead Polonius is thus in a sense 'with the king', but with the dead king, Hamlet's father, the king who is no longer with the body. With a further twist, the monarch that embodies the king, Hamlet's uncle, is nothing. For Hamlet, in this instance, the rules of philosophical ontology do not hold: the dead father is the king, while the living monarch is nothing.

The condition of the king as both thing and nothing is starkly revealed in the argument of *Richard II*. This play is central to the argument of Kantorowicz's understanding of the king's two bodies, which interprets the play in terms of an opposition between the two bodies of the temporal and the atemporal king. For Kantorowicz, the distinction between the king's two bodies allows for continuity of kingship across the lives of several, even competing kings. In this interpretation, the locus of temporal and atemporal kingship is the crown, which embodies kingship and can be worn by several consecutive kings or struggled for between contenders. There is no room for a hiatus or for nothing in this interpretation, for even when there is no king, there remains kingship. We have already seen that this distinction does not hold for *Hamlet*, which systematically exploits the ambiguity as to who is the king, not only in Kantorowicz's terms between the phenomenal and the essential king, but also between the living but illegitimate and the dead but legitimate 'king but not-king'. The same complexity informs *Richard II* where the equivocal character of nothing is the subject of the two reflections which form the axis of the play.

The first reflection takes place in II. ii. during the dialogue between Bushy and the queen following King Richard's confiscation of John of Gaunt's property and his departure for Ireland, catalysts of the events which would culminate in his deposition from the throne. The queen is melancholy, apprehensive that: 'Some unborn sorrow ripe in Fortune's womb / Is coming towards me, and my inward soul / With nothing trembles; at some thing it grieves / More than with parting from my lord the king' (*Richard II* II. ii.10–13). The queen's inward soul trembles with nothing, understood equivocally as a something that is more than the thing that is its apparent occasion. Bushy replies philosophically, reducing the queen's apprehension of nothing to the distinction between substance and accident. His argument is classically philosophical, anticipating Hegel's critique of abstract nothing in the *Logic*:

> Each substance of a grief hath twenty shadows,
> Which shows like grief itself, but is not so.
> For sorrow's eye, glazed with blinding tears,
> Divides one thing entire to many objects,
> Like perspectives, which, rightly gaz'd upon,
> Show nothing but confusion; ey'd awry,
> Distinguish form.

(II. ii. 14–20)

The substance of the queen's sorrow at the king's departure is anamorphically projected onto a number of different objects; her experience of dread at nothing is but a response to the confusion provoked by her projection of sorrow. By 'looking awry' at the king's departure, the queen will 'Find shapes of grief more than himself to wail' (II. ii. 22), but these are 'nought but shadows of what is not' – 'more's not seen, / Or if it be,'tis with false sorrow's eye' (II. ii. 23, 25–6). The nothing that causes dread in the queen is imaginary, an effect of anamorphic confusion; she should look instead to the substance of her grief which is indeed the king's departure.

The queen is not convinced by Bushy's philosophical explanation of her fear of nothing, and replies by evoking the sadness provoked by the paradox that to think of nothing is still a thought – to be full of nothing is still to be full: 'I cannot but be sad; so heavy sad, / As, though on thinking on no thought I think, / Makes me with heavy nothing faint and shrink' (II. ii. 30–2). The link between the queen's heavy sadness and the heavy nothing that provokes it is thought's negation of thought – which leaves nothing, but a nothing thought as if it were something. When the negation of thought is conceived as the thought of nothing, nothing takes on the contradictory characteristic of something thought, the depressing heaviness without qualities evoked by the queen. A half century after the composition of *Richard II*, Descartes would argue that thinking nothing was proof of the continuity of thought and of the being of the thinking subject. Thought's negation of itself was its ultimate affirmation. For Shakespeare, however, what is important is not the inference that can be drawn with respect to thought and the being of the thinking subject, but the equivocal character of nothing and the sadness it can provoke.

Bushy's reply to the queen's 'heavy nothing' is typical of the philosophical distaste for the equivocations of nothing: ''Tis nothing but conceit, my gracious lady' (II. ii. 33), but the queen is adamant. Conceit is derived from some object or past experience, whereas her dread is the issue of nothing: 'For nothing hath begot my sometime grief, / Or something hath the nothing that I grieve' (II. ii. 36–7). Far from being a conceit or rhetorical figure, the queen's nothing has the effect of grief and sadness; nothing has the uncanny quality of being experienced without being an object of experience; it has the effect of an object without being an object. Nothing is nameless, yet has a name: 'But what it is that is not yet known what, / I cannot name: 'tis nameless woe, I wot' (II. ii. 39–40). Nothing, then, is not nothing.

Acts IV and V of *Richard II*, in which King Richard is deposed by Bolingbroke, stage the king's recognition that he has become 'a thing of nothing'. To Bolingbroke's question whether he is content to resign the crown, Richard replies equivocally: 'Ay, no; no, ay; for I must nothing be. / Therefore no "no", for I resign to thee' (IV. i. 201–2). He acknowledges he must be nothing, but can neither affirm nor deny this nothing. His 'Ay' puns with the first person pronoun, making the 'Ay, no' read as an equivocation and as a definite refusal (I [resign the crown], no) while the following 'no, ay' reads as refusal and as resigned acquiescence. The pun on I and 'ay' continues in the next phrase in which what must nothing be is both the impossible affirmation, the 'ay' that would acquiesce in resigning the crown, and the I of the king which becomes nothing. When Richard does resign in the following line he does not acquiesce in the act by saying yes, but only gives a 'no "no"'. The latter is interpreted by all as an affirmation, but clearly for Richard the double negation denotes resignation and acquiesence, not affirmation and willing acceptance.

Later in the scene Richard requests a mirror in order to see his face 'bankrupt of majesty', and alludes back to the earlier scene with the queen when Bushy describes her grief as a substance that is distributed across several shadows giving the effect of nothing. Richard dashes the glass against the ground and cracks his face 'in an hundred shivers' (IV. i. 289). Unimpressed, Bolingbroke observes: 'The shadow of your sorrow hath destroy'd / The shadow of your face' (IV. i. 292–3). Richard takes this ironically as a lesson in philosophy – the 'substance' of his grief lies within – invisible and silent – shadowed in his outward laments and gestures. The latter, the shadows, are in Bolingbroke's view nothing, but in this case the substance too, being invisible and inexpressible, is also nothing. Bolingbroke's position is a platonic nihilism appropriate to a usurper – as substance can never fully appear through its accidents or 'shadows' so kingship is never fully manifest in the king – Richard's position is more complex, as appears in the final soliloquy that opens V. v.

In the soliloquy Richard experiences the decomposition of the metaphysics of kingship; it is not that he imperfectly embodies the substance of monarchy, but rather he has become the scene for any number of shifting identities: 'Thus play I in one person many people, / And none contented' (V. v. 31–2). The experience of decomposition leads him to reflect that the plethora of identities that throng across his stage are but shadows following the loss of the substance of kingship, and that he has become 'nothing'. This line of thought proceeds to the proposition: 'But whate'er I be, / Nor I, nor any man that but man is, / With nothing shall be pleas'd, till he be eas'd / With being nothing' (V. v. 38–41). Nothing here works in the same way as in Imogen's reply to the question 'What art thou?' in *Cymbeline*: 'I am nothing; or if not / Nothing to be were better' (IV. ii. 367–8). Neither Richard nor Imogen possesses a fixed identity, and in this they are nothing, but their nothingness is qualified by the thought of their nothing – their nothingness or negation of identity is negated to become not-nothing. They do not return to their previous identities, but inhabit a limbo which is neither being nor nothing. This spectral condition of not-nothing – characterized by the affects of grief and sorrow – is marked by the self-denying desire to 'be eased with being nothing' or 'nothing to be'.

The melancholic modality of nothing employed by Shakespeare in these instances performs the impossible condition that nothing be not-nothing. The issue of this condition – in spite of the desires of many commentators – is never an unconditional return to being or identity but the arrival at an inauthentic condition between being and nothing figured by Shakespeare as the stage or a scene peopled by actors. Yet alongside these melancholy monsters of nothing there is also an inspiring, productive nothing which operates across the figural and discursive orders. This is intimated in the histories around the figure of the crown, which in the form of a circle figures a hole, a well, but also a zero. The elision of nothing with the number zero as 'cipher' allows Shakespeare to develop an inventive concept of nothing. The basis of this conceit is that zero denotes nothing when added to a number in the mathematical operation of addition $(1 + 0 = 1)$, but multiplication by ten when it is placed to the right of a number $(1 + 0 = 10)$. Zero or 'cipher' by itself – without a figure – is nothing, as the Fool reminded Lear: 'thou art an O without a / figure; I am better than thou art now; I am a fool, thou / art nothing' (*King Lear* I. iv. 183–5), but when added to a figure, it multiplies it by ten: 'like a cipher / (Yet standing in rich place) I multiply / With one 'We thank you' many thousands moe / That go before it' (*The Winter's Tale* I. ii. 6–9). By placing zero beside a figure, something comes of nothing in spite of the maxim, but it is a thing of the imagination, neither unequivocal being nor nothing.

It is this property of nothing figured as zero which informs the conceit of the Prologue to *Henry V*. The opening peroration: 'O, for a muse of fire, that would ascend / The brightest heaven of invention; / A kingdom for a stage, princes to act / And monarchs to behold the swelling scene!' (Prologue, 1–4) is followed by an apology for the 'flat unraised spirits' of the actors and 'unworthy scaffold' (9–10) of the stage. The contrast between the 'swelling scene' and the 'miserable scaffold' is eased by the muse of fire, which is nothing, the vocative 'O' of the peroration. The muse of fire is itself 'O' or nothing, as Shakespeare then spells out in an elaborate conceit on nothing and the figure zero. First of all, the Globe itself is nothing – 'may we cram / Within this wooden O the very casques / That did affright the air at Agincourt?' (12–14) and then the actors themselves are the crooked figures beside which the Prologue places the ciphers or zeros of the imagination: 'O, pardon! since a crooked figure may / Attest in little place a million; / And let us, ciphers to this great accompt, / On your imaginary forces work' (15–18). What comes out of this nothing is not the real event of the battle of

Agincourt, but an illusion, not nothing but a thing of the imagination which has its own reality yet which is not being.

Shakespeare's monster of nothing emphasizes paradox, ignoring the logic of non-contradiction and delaying the passage from nothing to being. The monster of nothing exploits logical contradiction to other ends, above all those of affect and the experience of time. Whenever Shakespeare plays with the equivocation of nothing, it is to express sorrow, guilt or love and the experience of the passing of time. These affects and the experience of time are not shadows of a substance, nor affirmations of some state of being, whether present in the past or to come, but rather paradoxical experiences which cannot be contained by philosophical categories. Shakespeare's monster of nothing pits equivocation against the unequivocal categories of philosophical ontology, showing how the experience of not-nothing – the experience of the deposed monarch, the imaginary sorrow of Queen Isabel, the desire not to be of Imogen, and the inventions of the muse of fire – cannot be reduced to unequivocal states of being. To Benedict's sincere but facile profession in *Much Ado About Nothing* – 'I do love nothing in the world so well as you – is / not that strange?' (IV. i. 266) – Beatrice replies by showing the equivocation in his unequivocal declaration: 'As strange as the thing I know not. It were as / possible for me to say I loved nothing so well as you, / but believe me not; and yet I lie not; I confess / nothing, nor I deny nothing' (IV. i. 267–71).

Notes

1 Shakespeare frequently gives 'monster' the sense of to present or to show in an exaggerated form, as in Coriolanus's rebuke: 'I had rather have one scratch my head I'th'sun / When the alarum were struck, than idly sit / To hear my nothings monster'd' (*Coriolanus* II. ii. 75–8).
2 The properties of such elisions have been admirably analysed by Jean-François Lyotard in *Discours, figur* (1971).

Bibliography

Adamson, James (1844) *Modern Literature*, Cape Town: J. C. Collard.

Adorno, T. W. (1984) *Aesthetic Theory*, trans. C. Lenhardt, London: Routledge & Kegan Paul.

—— (1990) *Negative Dialectics*, trans. E. B. Ashton, London: Routledge.

Althusser, Louis (1971) 'Ideology and ideological state apparatuses: notes towards an investigation', in his *Lenin and Philosophy and Other Essays*, trans. Ben Brewster, New York: Monthly Review Press, 127–86.

—— (1977) *For Marx*, trans. Ben Brewster, London: New Left Books.

Appiah, Kwame Anthony (1992) *In My Father's House: Africa in the Philosophy of Culture*, New York: Oxford University Press.

Ashton, Rosemary (1980) *The German Idea: Four English Writers and the Reception of German Thought, 1800–1860*, Cambridge: Cambridge University Press.

Attridge, Derek (1999) 'Innovation, literature, ethics: relating to the other', *PMLA* 114, 1: 20–31.

Balibar, Etienne and Macherey, Pierre (1981) 'On literature as an ideological form', in *Untying the Text: A Post-Structuralist Reader*, ed. Robert Young, London: Routledge & Kegan Paul, 79–99.

Bank, Andrew (1995) 'Liberals and their enemies: Racial ideology at the Cape of Good Hope, 1820–1850', unpublished Ph.D. thesis, University of Cambridge.

Barker, Francis (1984) *The Tremulous Private Body: Essays on Subjection*, London: Methuen.

Bataille, Georges (1985) *Visions of Excess: Selected Writings, 1927–1939*, ed. Allan Stoekl, trans. Allan Stoekl, Carl R. Lovitt and Donald M. Leslie, Jr, Minneapolis: University of Minnesota Press.

—— (1992) *On Nietzsche*, trans. B. Boone, New York: Paragon House.

Bate, Jonathan (1986) *Shakespeare and the English Romantic Imagination*, Oxford: Clarendon.

—— (1992) 'Shakespeare and original genius', in *Genius: The History of an Idea*, ed. Penelope Murray, Oxford: Blackwell, 76–97.

—— (1997) *The Genius of Shakespeare*, London: Picador.

Baudrillard, Jean (1986) 'The precession of simulacra', in *Art After Modernism: Rethinking Representation*, ed. Brian Wallis, trans. Paul Foss and Paul Patton, New York: The New Museum of Contemporary Art, 253–81.

—— (1993) *The Transparency of Evil: Essays on Extreme Phenomena*, trans. James Benedict, London and New York: Verso.

Belsey, Catherine (1980) *Critical Practice*, London: Methuen.

—— (1985) *The Subject of Tragedy: Identity and Difference in Renaissance Drama*, London: Methuen.

Benjamin, Walter (1979) 'Critique of violence', in his *One Way Street and Other Writings*, trans. Edmund Jephcott and Kingsley Shorter, London: NLB, 132–54.

Bennett, Andrew and Royle, Nicholas (1999) *An Introduction to Literature, Criticism and Theory*, Hemel Hempstead: Prentice Hall Europe.

Bernstein, J. M. (1992) *The Fate of Art: Aesthetic Alienation from Kant to Derrida and Adorno*, Oxford: Polity Press.

Bewes, Timothy (1997) *Cynicism and Postmodernity*, London and New York: Verso.

Bloom, Harold (1999) *Shakespeare: The Invention of the Human*, London: Fourth Estate Limited.

Borch-Jacobsen, Mikkel (1991) *Lacan: The Absolute Master*, trans. Douglas Brick, Stanford: Stanford University Press.

Botting, Fred and Wilson, Scott (eds) (1997a) *The Bataille Reader*, Oxford: Blackwell.

—— (1997b) 'Pow pow pow Hamlet, Bataille and Marxism now', *parallax* 4: 119–36.

—— (1998) *Bataille: A Critical Reader*, Oxford: Blackwell.

Bowie, Andrew (1990) *Aesthetics and Subjectivity: From Kant to Nietzsche*, Manchester: Manchester University Press.

—— (1997) *From Romanticism to Critical Theory: The Philosophy of German Literary Theory*, London: Routledge.

Bradley, A. C. (1992) *Shakespearean Tragedy: Lectures on Hamlet, Othello, King Lear and Macbeth*, 3rd edn, introd. John Russell Brown, London: Macmillan.

Brink, André (1996) *Destabilising Shakespeare*, Grahamstown: Shakespeare Society of Southern Africa.

Bristol, Michael (1996) *Big-time Shakespeare*, London and New York: Routledge.

Bruns, Gerald (1990) 'Stanley Cavell's Shakespeare', *Critical Inquiry* 16: 612–32.

Bruster, Douglas (1992) *Drama and the Market in the Age of Shakespeare*, Cambridge: Cambridge University Press.

Buck-Morss, Susan (1977) *The Origin of Negative Dialectics: Theodor W. Adorno, Walter Benjamin and the Frankfurt Institute*, New York: Macmillan.

Bullock, Marcus Paul (1987) *Romanticism and Marxism: The Philosophical Development of Literary Theory and Literary History in Walter Benjamin and Friedrich Schlegel*, New York: Peter Lang.

Butler, Judith (1990) *Gender Trouble: Feminism and the Subversion of Identity*, London and New York: Routledge.

—— (1993) *Bodies that Matter: On the Discursive Limits of 'Sex'*, London and New York: Routledge.

—— (1997) *Excitable Speech: A Politics of the Performative*, London and New York: Routledge.

Caldwell, Ellen C. (1995) 'Jack Cade and Shakespeare's *Henry VI, Part 2*', *Studies in Philology* 92, 1: 18–79.

Cartelli, Thomas (1994) 'Jack Cade in the garden: class consciousness and class conflict in *2 Henry VI*', in *Enclosure Acts: Sexuality, Property, and Culture in Early Modern England*, ed. Richard Burt and John Michael Archer, Ithaca: Cornell University Press, 48–67.

Cavell, Stanley (1969) *Must We Mean What We Say?*, Cambridge: Cambridge University Press.

—— (1987) *Disowning Knowledge: In Six Plays of Shakespeare*, Cambridge: Cambridge University Press.

—— (1998) 'Skepticism as iconoclasm', in *Shakespeare and the Twentieth Century: The Selected Proceedings of the International Shakespeare Association, World Congress, Los Angeles, 1996*, ed. Jonathan Bate, Jill L. Levenson and Dieter Mehl, Newark: University of Delaware Press, 231–47.

Caygill, Howard (1993) 'Violence, civility and the predicaments of philosophy', in *The Political Subject of Violence*, ed. David Campbell and Michael Dillon, Manchester: Manchester University Press, 48–72.

Charnes, Linda (1993) *Notorious Identity: Materializing the Subject in Shakespeare*, Cambridge, Mass.: Harvard University Press.

—— (1997) 'Dismember me: Shakespeare, paranoia, and the logic of mass culture', *Shakespeare Quarterly* 48, 1: 1–16.

Colchester, Henry Billiter (1926) 'Memoir of Bishop Merriman', in *Republic of Cluny Annual Register and Miscellany for 1926*, vol. 3, pt. 1, no. 15: 54–87.

'Colonial extracts', *Anglo-African* (3 September 1857), 3, 216: 2–4.

'Colonial extracts', *Anglo-African*, (12 November 1857), 3, 226: 4.

Copjec, Joan (1994) *Read My Desire: Lacan against the Historicists*, Cambridge, Mass.: MIT Press.

Critchley, Simon (1998) 'Introduction: what is Continental philosophy', in *A Companion to Continental Philosophy*, ed. Simon Critchley and William R. Schroeder, Oxford: Blackwell, 1–17.

Critchley, Simon and Dews, Peter (eds) (1996) *Deconstructive Subjectivities*, New York: State University of New York.

Currie, Gregory (1990) *The Nature of Fiction*, Cambridge: Cambridge University Press.

de Grazia, Margreta (1991) *Shakespeare Verbatim: The Reproduction of Authenticity and the 1790 Apparatus*, Oxford: Clarendon Press.

Deleuze, Gilles (1983) *Nietzsche and Philosophy*, trans. H. Tomlinson, London: Athlone Press.

—— (1985) 'Nomad thought', in *The New Nietzsche*, ed. D. B. Allison, Cambridge, Mass.: MIT Press, 142–9.

—— (1994) *Difference and Repetition*, trans. P. Patton, London: Athlone Press.

—— (1995) *Negotiations 1972–1990*, trans. Martin Joughin, New York: Columbia University Press.

Deleuze, Gilles and Guattari, Félix (1972) *Anti-Oedipus: Capitalism and Schizophrenia*, trans. Robert Hurley, Mark Seem and Helen R. Lane, Minneapolis: University of Minnesota Press.

—— (1988) *A Thousand Plateaus: Capitalism and Schizophrenia*, trans. Brian Massumi, London: Athlone Press.

de Man, Paul (1984) *The Rhetoric of Romanticism*, New York: Columbia University Press.

Derrida, Jacques (1978) 'The theater of cruelty and the closure of representation', in his *Writing and Difference*, trans. Alan Bass, Chicago: University of Chicago Press, 232–50.

—— (1981) 'Economimesis', trans. R. Klein, *Diacritics* 11, 2: 3–25.

—— (1992) 'Force of law: the "mystical foundation of authority" ', in *Deconstruction and the Possibility of Justice*, ed. Drucilla Cornell, Michel Rosenfeld and David Gray Carlson, New York and London: Routledge, 3–67.

—— (1994) *Specters of Marx: The State of the Debt, the Work of Mourning, and the New International*, trans. Peggy Kamuf, New York and London: Routledge.

—— (1995) *The Gift of Death*, trans. D. Wills, Chicago and London: University of Chicago Press.

—— (1998) 'From restricted to general economy: a Hegelianism without reserve', in Botting and Wilson (1998), 102–38.

Dews, Peter (1987) *Logics of Disintegration: Post-Structuralist Thought and the Claims of Critical Theory*, London: Verso.

—— (1995) *The Limits of Disenchantment: Essays on Contemporary European Philosophy*, London: Verso.

Dobson, Michael (1992) *The Making of the National Poet: Shakespeare Adaptation and Authorship, 1660–1769*, Oxford: Oxford University Press.

Dollimore, Jonathan (1984) *Radical Tragedy: Religion, Ideology, and Power in the Drama of Shakespeare and his Contemporaries*, London: Harvester, 2nd edn 1989.

Dollimore, Jonathan and Sinfield, Alan (eds) (1985) *Political Shakespeare: New Essays in Cultural Materialism*, Manchester: Manchester University Press, 2nd edn 1994.

Drakakis, John (ed.) (1985) *Alternative Shakespeares*, London: Methuen.

Dumézil, G. (1988) *Mitra-Varuna*, trans. Derek Coltman, New York: Zone Books.

Eagleton, Terry (1986) *William Shakespeare*, Oxford: Basil Blackwell.

—— (1990) *The Ideology of the Aesthetic*, Oxford: Basil Blackwell.

Easthope, Antony (1988) *British Post-Structuralism: Since 1968*, London: Routledge.

Elliott, Gregory (ed.) (1994) *Althusser: A Critical Reader*, Oxford: Blackwell.

Emerson, Ralph Waldo (1883) *Representative Men: Seven Lectures*, London: George Routledge & Sons.

Fineman, Joel (1989) 'The history of the anecdote: fiction and fiction', in Aram H. Veeser (1989), 49–76.

Fletcher, A. (1964) *Allegory: The Theory of a Symbolic Mode*, Ithaca: Cornell University Press.

Foucault, Michel (1970) *The Order of Things: An Archaeology of the Human Sciences*, trans. Alan Sheridan, London: Tavistock.

—— (1977) *Language, Counter-Memory, Practice*, ed. D. F. Bouchard, Ithaca: Cornell University Press.

—— (1979) *Discipline and Punish: The Birth of the Prison*, trans. Alan Sheridan, New York: Vintage.

—— (1986) *The Care of the Self*, vol. 3: *The History of Sexuality*, trans. Robert Hurley, New York: Vintage.

—— (1998) 'A preface to transgression', in Botting and Wilson (1998), 24–40.

Giddens, Anthony (1991) *Modernity and Self-Identity: Self and Society in the Late Modern Age*, Stanford: Stanford University Press.

Girouard, M. (1980) *Life in an English Country House: A Social and Architectural History*, Harmondsworth: Penguin.

Gould, Timothy (1992) 'Cavell, Stanley', in *A Companion to Aesthetics*, ed. D. Cooper, J. Margolis and C. Sartwell, Oxford: Blackwell, 63–6.

Goux, Jean-Joseph (1998) 'General economics and postmodern capitalism', in Botting and Wilson (1998), 196–213.

Grady, Hugh (1991) *The Modernist Shakespeare: Critical Texts in a Material World*, Oxford: Clarendon.

—— (1993) 'Containment, subversion – and postmodernism', *Textual Practice* 7, 1: 31–49.

—— (1996) *Shakespeare's Universal Wolf: Studies in Early Modern Reification*, Oxford: Clarendon.

—— (1998) 'Further notes on Marxism(s) and the lyric', in *New Definitions of Lyric: Theoretical and Critical Essays*, ed. Mark Jeffreys, New York: Garland, 179–200.

Greenblatt, Stephen J. (1980) *Renaissance Self-fashioning: From More to Shakespeare*, Chicago: University of Chicago Press.

—— (1997) 'What is the history of literature', *Critical Inquiry* 23: 460–81.

Habermas, Jürgen (1979) *Knowledge and Human Interests*, trans. Jeremy Shapiro, Boston: Beacon.

—— (1984, 1987a) *The Theory of Communicative Action*, trans. Thomas McCarthy, 2 vols, Boston: Beacon.

—— (1987b) *The Philosophical Discourse of Modernity*, trans. Frederick Lawrence, Cambridge, Mass.: MIT Press.

—— (1992) *The Structural Transformation of the Public Sphere: An Inquiry into a Category of Bourgeois Society*, trans. Thomas Burger with the assistance of Frederick Lawrence, Oxford: Polity Press.

Halpern, R. (1991) *The Poetics of Primitive Accumulation: English Renaissance Culture and the Genealogy of Capital*, Ithaca and London: Cornell University Press.

Hawkes, Terence (1985) '*Telmah*', in Parker and Hartman (1985), 310–32.

—— (ed.) (1996) *Alternative Shakespeares*, vol. 2, London and New York, Routledge.

Hegel, G. W. F. (1969) *The Science of Logic*, trans. A. V. Miller, London: George Allen & Unwin.

Heidegger, Martin (1987) *An Introduction to Metaphysics*, trans. Ralph Manheim, New Haven and London: Yale University Press.

Held, David (1980) *Introduction to Critical Theory: Horkheimer to Habermas*, Berkeley: University of California Press.

Helmholtz-Phelan, A. A. (1971) *The Indebtedness of Samuel Taylor Coleridge to August Wilhelm von Schlegel*, New York: Haskell House.

Hibbard, G. R. (ed.) (1987) *Hamlet*, Oxford: Clarendon Press.

Holderness, Graham (1987) *Hamlet* (Open Guides to Literature Series), Milton Keynes, UK: Open University Press.

Horkheimer, Max (1972) 'Authority and the family', in *Critical Theory: Selected Essays*, trans. M. J. O'Connell, New York: Seabury, 47–128.

Horkheimer, Max and Adorno, T. W. (1972) *Dialectic of Enlightenment*, trans. John Cumming, Boston: Seabury.

Irigaray, Luce (1991) *Marine Lover of Friedrich Nietzsche*, trans. Gillian C. Gill, New York: Columbia University Press.

James, Henry (1964) 'The birthplace', in *The Complete Tales of Henry James*, vol. 11: *1900–1903*, ed. Leon Edel, London: Rupert Hart-Davis Ltd, 403–65.

—— (1981) *Selected Literary Criticism*, ed. Morris Shapira, Cambridge: Cambridge University Press.

Jameson, Fredric (1971) *Marxism and Form: Twentieth-Century Dialectical Theories of Literature*, Princeton, NJ: Princeton University Press.

—— (1972) *The Prison-House of Language: A Critical Account of Structuralism and Russian Formalism*, Princeton, NJ: Princeton University Press.

—— (1981) *The Political Unconscious: Narrative as a Socially Symbolic Act*, Ithaca, NY: Cornell University Press.

—— (1990) *Late Marxism: Adorno, or the Persistence of the Dialectic*, London: Verso.

—— (1991) *Postmodernism, or, The Cultural Logic of Late Capitalism*, Durham: Duke University Press.

Jay, Martin (1973) *The Dialectical Imagination: A History of the Frankfurt School and the Institute of Social Research, 1923–1950*, Boston: Little, Brown.

—— (1984a) *Adorno*, Cambridge, Mass.: Harvard University Press.

—— (1984b) *Marxism and Totality: The Adventures of a Concept from Lukács to Habermas*, Berkeley: University of California Press.

Johnson, S. (1969) *Johnson on Shakespeare*, ed. W. K. Wimsatt, Harmondsworth: Penguin.

Jonson, Ben (1966) *Three Comedies*, ed. Michael Jamieson, Harmondsworth: Penguin.

Kamps, Ivo (ed.) (1991) *Shakespeare Left and Right*, New York and London: Routledge.

Kant, Immanuel (1983) 'An answer to the question: what is enlightenment?', in his *Perpetual Peace and Other Essays*, trans. Ted Humphrey, Indianapolis and Cambridge: Hackett Publishing Co., 40–8.

Kantorowicz, Ernst (1957) *The King's Two Bodies: A Study in Mediaeval Political Theology*, Princeton: Princeton University Press.

Kellner, Douglas (1989) *Critical Theory, Marxism, and Modernity*, Baltimore: Johns Hopkins University Press.

Kerrigan, William (1998) 'The case for bardolatry: Harold Bloom rescues Shakespeare from the critics', *Lingua Franca* 8, 8: 28–37.

Klossowski, Pierre (1997) *Nietzsche and the Vicious Circle*, trans. Daniel W. Smith, London: Athlone Press.

Knights, L. C. (1946) 'How many children had Lady Macbeth?', in his *Explorations: Essays in Criticism, Mainly on the Literature of the Seventeenth Century*, London: Chatto & Windus, 1–39.

Kojève, A. (1969) *Introduction to the Reading of Hegel*, assembled by R. Queneau, ed. A. Bloom, trans. J. H. Nichols, Jr, Ithaca: Cornell University Press.

Lacan, Jacques (1977a) *Écrits: A Selection*, trans. Alan Sheridan, London: Routledge.

—— (1977b) 'Desire and the interpretation of desire in *Hamlet*', trans. James Hulbert, *Yale French Studies* 55/56: 11–52.

—— (1979) *The Four Fundamental Concepts of Psychoanalysis*, trans. Alan Sheridan, Harmondsworth: Penguin.

—— (1981) 'God and the *jouissance* of the woman', in *Feminine Sexuality: Jacques Lacan and the école freudienne*, ed. Juliet Mitchell and Jacqueline Rose, London: Macmillan, 137–48.

—— (1991a) *The Seminar of Jacques Lacan*, Book I: *Freud's Papers on Technique 1953–1954*, ed. Jacques-Alain Miller, trans. John Forrester, New York and London: Norton.

—— (1991b) *The Seminar of Jacques Lacan*, Book II: *The Ego in Freud's Theory and in the Technique of Psychoanalysis 1954–1955*, ed. Jacques-Alain Miller, trans. Sylvana Tomaselli, New York and London: Norton.

—— (1992) *The Seminar of Jacques Lacan*, Book VII: *The Ethics of Psychoanalysis, 1959–1960*, trans. D. Porter, London: Routledge.

Lacoue-Labathe, Philippe and Nancy, Jean-Luc (1986) *The Literary Absolute: The Theory of Literature in German Romanticism*, trans. Philip Barnard and Cheryl Lister, New York: State University of New York Press.

Land, Nick (1992) *The Thirst for Annihilation*, London: Routledge.

—— (1993) 'Machinic desire', *Textual Practice* 7, 3: 471–82.

Laqueur, Thomas (1990) *Making Sex: Body and Gender from the Greeks to Freud*, Cambridge, Mass.: Harvard University Press.

Latour, Bruno (1993) *We Have Never Been Modern*, trans. Catherine Porter, Cambridge, Mass.: Harvard University Press.

Lewis, David (1983) 'Truth in fiction', in his *Philosophical Papers*, vol. I, Oxford: Oxford University Press, 261–80.

Loomba, Ania and Orkin, Martin (eds) (1998) *Postcolonial Shakespeares*, London and New York: Routledge.

Lukács, Georg (1974) 'Legality and illegality', in his *History and Class Consciousness*, trans. Rodney Livingstone, London: Merlin, 256–71.

Lyons, Donald (1999) 'Bardolatry', *Commentary* 107, 4: 53–6.

Lyotard, Jean-François (1971) *Discours, figur*, Paris: Klincksieck.

Macey, David (1994) 'Thinking with borrowed concepts: Althusser and Lacan', in Gregory Elliott (1994), 142–58.

—— (1995) *The Lives of Michel Foucault*, New York: Vintage.

McGee, A. (1987) *The Elizabethan Hamlet*, New Haven and London: Yale University Press.

Marcuse, Herbert (1977) *Reason and Revolution*, London: Routledge & Kegan Paul.

Marx, Karl (1968) *The Communist Manifesto*, New York: Monthly Review Press.

Marx, Karl and Engels, F. (1947) *The German Ideology*, ed. R. Pascal, New York: International.

Merriman, Nathaniel (1857) *On the Study of Shakespeare*, Grahamstown, South Africa: The General Institute.

—— (1858) *Shakespeare as Bearing on English History*, Grahamstown, South Aftrica: The General Institute.

—— (1876) *Are the Missionaries Mischief-Workers?*, Grahamstown, South Africa: H. Guest & Son.

Middleton, Peter (1998) 'Does literary theory give you a sense of *déjà vu.?*', *Textual Practice* 12, 1: 148–63.

Miller, J. Hillis (1987) 'Presidential address 1986: the triumph of theory, the resistance to reading, and the question of the material base', *PMLA* 102: 281–91.

Mudimbe, V. Y. (1988) *The Invention of Africa: Gnosis, Philosophy, and the Order of Things*, Bloomington: Indiana University Press.

Mullaney, Steven (1996) 'After the new historicism', in Terence Hawkes (1996), 17–37.

Nancy, Jean-Luc (1997) 'The insufficiency of "values" and the necessity of "sense"', trans. Steve Bastow, *Cultural Values* 1, 1: 127–31.

Nietzsche, Friedrich (1968) *The Will to Power*, trans. Walter Kaufmann and R. J. Hollingdale, New York: Vintage Books.

—— (1969) *On the Genealogy of Morals and Ecce Homo*, trans. Walter Kaufmann and R. J. Hollingdale, New York: Vintage Books.

—— (1974) *The Gay Science*, trans. Walter Kaufmann, New York: Vintage Books.

—— (1983) *Untimely Meditations*, trans. R. J. Hollingdale, Cambridge: Cambridge University Press.

—— (1984) *Beyond Good and Evil*, trans. R. J. Hollingdale, Harmondsworth: Penguin.

Norris, Christopher (1994) *Truth and the Ethics of Criticism*, Manchester: Manchester University Press.

'Notes of the week', *Grahamstown Journal* (26 April 1856), 25, 1268: 4.

'Notes of the week', *Grahamstown Journal* (5 September 1857), 27, 1396: 4.

'Notes of the week', *Grahamstown Journal* (7 November 1857), 27, 1413: 4.

Nuttall, A. D. (1999) 'Harold Bloom's Shakespeare', *Raritan* 18, 3: 123–34.

Oruka, Henry (1990) *Trends in Contemporary African Philosophy*, Nairobi: Shirikon.

Parker, Patricia and Hartman, Geoffrey (eds) (1985) *Shakespeare and the Question of Theory*, London: Methuen.

Patterson, Annabel (1989) *Shakespeare and the Popular Voice*, Oxford: Basil Blackwell.

Peires, Jeff (1989) *The Dead Will Arise: Nongqawuse and the Great Xhosa Cattle-Killing Movement of 1856–7*, Johannesburg: Ravan.

Pipkin, James (ed.) (1985) *English and German Romanticism: Cross-Currents and Controversies*, Heidelberg: Carl Winter.

Rabkin, Norman (1967) *Shakespeare and the Common Understanding*, London: Macmillan.

Ragland-Sullivan, E. (1987) *Jacques Lacan and the Philosophy of Psychoanalysis*, Urbana, Ill.: University of Illinois Press.

Raulet, G. (1983) 'Structuralism and post-structuralism: an interview with Michel Foucault', *Telos* 55: 195–211.

'Relief for India', *Anglo-African* (12 November 1857), 3, 226: 4.

Rockmore, Tom (1995) *Heidegger and French Philosophy: Humanism, Antihumanism, and Being*, London and New York: Routledge.

Rose, Gillian (1978) *The Melancholy Science: An Introduction to the Thought of Theodor W. Adorno*, New York: Columbia University Press.

—— (1992) *The Broken Middle: Out of our Ancient Society*, Oxford: Blackwell.

—— (1995) *Love's Work*, London: Chatto & Windus.

Sauer, Thomas (1981) *A. W. Schlegel's Shakespearean Criticism in England, 1811– 1846*, Bonn: Bouvier Verlag Herbert Grundman.

Schiller, F. (1967) *On the Aesthetic Education of Man in a Series of Letters*, ed. and trans. E. M. Wilkinson and L. A. Willoughby, Oxford: Clarendon Press.

Schlegel, A. W. (1846) *A Course of Lectures on Dramatic Art and Literature*, trans. John Black, London: Henry G. Bohn.

Schlegel, Friedrich (1996) 'Essay on the concept of republicanism occasioned by the Kantian tract *Perpetual Peace*', in *The Early Political Writings of the German Romantics*, ed. Frederick C. Beiser, trans. Frederick C. Beiser, Cambridge: Cambridge University Press, 93–112.

Scruton, Roger (1999) 'Defining moments', *Sunday Times* (culture section), 1 August 1999.

Serequeberhan, Tsenay (1991) *African Philosophy: The Essential Readings*, New York: Paragon.

Shakespeare, William (1969) *2 Henry VI*, ed. Andrew Cairncross, London: Methuen.

—— (1981) *Richard III*, ed. Antony Hammond, London: Methuen.

—— (1982) *The Winter's Tale*, ed. J. H. P. Pafford, London: Methuen.

—— (1985) *Julius Caesar*, ed. T. S. Dorsch, London: Methuen.

—— (1987) *Coriolanus*, ed. Philip Brockbank, London: Methuen.

—— (1988) *Much Ado about Nothing*, ed. A. R. Humphreys, London: Routledge.

—— (1990) *Hamlet*, ed. Harold Jenkins, London: Routledge.

—— (1991) *Richard II*, ed. Peter Ure, London: Routledge.

—— (1993) *Henry V*, ed. John H. Walter, London: Routledge.

—— (1994) *Cymbeline*, ed. J. M. Noseworthy, London: Routledge.

—— (1997) *Macbeth*, ed. Kenneth Muir, Walton-on-Thames: Thomas Nelson & Sons Ltd.

—— (1998) *King Lear*, ed. R. A. Foakes, Walton-on-Thames: Thomas Nelson & Sons Ltd.

Sinfield, Alan (1992) *Faultlines: Cultural Materialism and the Politics of Dissident Reading*, Oxford: Oxford University Press.

Sloterdijk, Peter (1987) *Critique of Cynical Reason*, trans. Michael Eldred, Minneapolis: University of Minnesota Press.

Speake, Jennifer (ed.) (1979) *A Dictionary of Philosophy*, London: Macmillan.

Stallybrass, Peter (1996) '*Macbeth* and witchcraft', in *Shakespeare's Late Tragedies: A Collection of Critical Essays*, ed. Susanne L. Wofford, Upper Saddle River, NJ: Prentice Hall, 104–18.

Strohm, Paul (1996) 'The trouble with Richard: the reburial of Richard II and Lancastrian symbolic strategy', *Speculum* 71: 87–111.

Studies in Romanticism (Special Issue on Walter Benjamin) (1992) 31, 4.

Taylor, Charles (1989) *Sources of the Self: The Making of the Modern Identity*, Cambridge, Mass.: Harvard University Press.

Taylor, Gary (1990) *Re-inventing Shakespeare*, London: The Hogarth Press.

Thompson, E. P. (1966) *The Making of the English Working Class*, New York: Vintage.

Varley, D. H. and Matthew, H. M. (eds) (1957) *The Cape Journals of Archdeacon N. J. Merriman 1848–1855*, Cape Town: Van Riebeeck Society.

Veeser, Aram H. (ed.) (1989) *The New Historicism*, New York and London: Routledge.

Vickers, Brian (1995) *The Critical Heritage 1623–1801*, 6 vols, London: Routledge.

Walton, Kendall (1990) *Mimesis as Make-Believe: On the Foundations of the Representational Arts*, Cambridge, Mass.: Harvard University Press.

wa Thiong'o, Ngugi (1993) *Moving the Center: The Struggle for Cultural Freedoms*, London: Heinemann.

Wells, Stanley (1999) ' "Millennium Masterworks": Shakespeare', *Sunday Times* (culture section), 15 August 1999.

Whibley, Pauline Megan (1982) *Merriman of Grahamstown*, Cape Town: Howard Timmins.

Wiggershaus, Rolf (1994) *The Frankfurt School: Its History, Theories and Political Significance*, trans. Michael Robertson, Oxford: Polity Press.

Wilks, J. S. (1990) *The Idea of Conscience in Renaissance Tragedy*, London and New York: Routledge.

Wilson, Richard (1986) ' "A mingled yarn": Shakespeare and the cloth workers', *Literature and History* 12, 2: 164–80.

—— (1992) *Julius Caesar*, Harmondsworth: Penguin.

Wilson, Scott (1992) 'Love and the labyrinth', *Assays* VII: 43–70.

—— (1995) *Cultural Materialism: Theory and Practice*, Oxford: Blackwell.

Wilson, W. Daniel (1989) '*Philosophen- und Schriftstellerkabale*: the conspiracy theory of the French revolution and the origins of German Romanticism (Fichte, F. Schlegel, Novalis)', *Euphorion* 83, 2: 131–59.

Wittgenstein, Ludwig (1994) *Culture and Value*, ed. G. H. Von Wright in collaboration with Heikki Nyman, trans. Peter Winch, Oxford: Blackwell.

Wood, David (ed.) (1990) *Philosophers' Poets*, London and New York, Routledge.

Žižek, Slavoj (1989) *The Sublime Object of Ideology*, London and New York: Verso.

—— (1992) *Enjoy Your Symptom: Jacques Lacan in Hollywood and Out*, New York and London: Routledge.

—— (1993) *Tarrying with the Negative: Kant, Hegel, and the Critique of Ideology*, Durham: Duke University Press.

Index

Learning Resources
Centre